# ADVANCED
# PSYCHOLOGY

Contemporary Topics

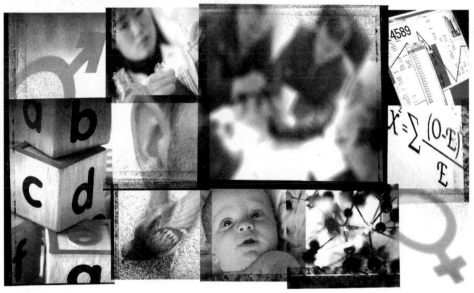

# ADVANCED
# PSYCHOLOGY
## Contemporary Topics

Pete Houghton and Dave Robinson

## Hodder & Stoughton
A MEMBER OF THE HODDER HEADLINE GROUP

Orders: please contact Bookpoint Ltd, 130 Milton Park, Abingdon, Oxon OX14 4SB.
Telephone: (44) 01235 827720. Fax: (44) 01235 400454. Lines are open from 9.00 – 6.00,
Monday to Saturday, with a 24 hour message answering service. You can also order through our website
www.hodderheadline.co.uk.

British Library Cataloguing in Publication Data
A catalogue record for this title is available from the British Library

ISBN 0 340 859326

First Published 2003
Impression number     10 9 8 7 6 5 4 3 2 1
Year                  2009 2008 2007 2006 2005 2004 2003

Typeset by Dorchester Typesetting Group Limited.
Printed in Great Britain for Hodder & Stoughton Educational, a division of Hodder Headline Plc,
338 Euston Road, London  NW1 3BH by J.W. Arrowsmith Ltd, Bristol

# Contents

# How to use this book

This book has been designed to meet the needs of students and teachers studying for the Contemporary Topics option in Module 4 of the AQA A2 level (Specification B) in Psychology.

Each chapter in this book provides short descriptions of empirical studies and experiments directly related to the topic areas. There are also some small group and individual activities to try. It is recommended that you carry out as many of these as possible since they will help you with remembering material and thinking more deeply and critically about psychology. The chapters offer numerous evaluative comments that will help you to analyse, discuss and make application of theory, concepts and research. This will help you gain AO2 marks (for evaluation and application) in the examination.

Each chapter contains four different types of learning activities as follows:

**Reflective Activity**   This invites you to engage in a reflective activity. This gives you something to think about before continuing with your reading.

**Practical Activity**   This invites you to conduct some kind of practical activity. Here a suggestion is made that may be either carried out on your own or with a small group of people. Some activities will take time outside of reading further in the chapter.

**Study**   This indicates that a study or experiment in psychology is described. Studies have been selected that are important and/or highlight theory or key concepts in psychology. The study or experiment is presented in the way required when you are asked to describe a study in an examination question. When reading the study try to identify strengths and shortcomings, and think about ways in which the study could be improved.

**Evaluative Comment**   This indicates an evaluative comment. These provide you with critical comment and analysis. Try to elaborate on the point being made, or use the comment as a basis for a small group discussion to explore other points of view. The skills of evaluation and analysis are essential to the study of psychology and are needed if you wish to gain high grades. Evaluative comments help with the second assessment objective (AO2) examined throughout the AS and A level in psychology.

Towards the end of each chapter you will find a number of questions. These have been set in the style that appears in the AQA Specification B A2 examinations. Each question shows the number of marks available and the marks for the 2 assessment objectives. Assessment objective 1 (AO1) is concerned with knowledge and understanding. Assessment objective 2 (AO2) is concerned with critical evaluation, analysis and application of theory.

At the end of each chapter you will find a list of suggestions for further reading. This is divided into two parts, first introductory books and then more specialist texts. The introductory texts should be easily accessible to all students. The specialist books are more demanding and will be of particular value to students who wish to achieve high grades. Some relevant and accessible websites are also listed.

*Pete Houghton and Dave Robinson*
*2003*

# Acknowledgements

The authors would like to thank Emma Woolf and Jasmine Brown at Hodder & Stoughton and Donald Pennington for guidance, advice and support in developing and producing this book. Thanks also to Rachel O'Connor for proof reading the text.

**Dave Robinson:** special thanks to Sarah D for the smiles and keeping it real!

**Pete Houghton:** for her patience and for being there, thank you, Jane. I would like to dedicate my chapters to the Social Sciences staff at Wigan and Leigh College; soon to be colleagues no more, but I hope, always friends.

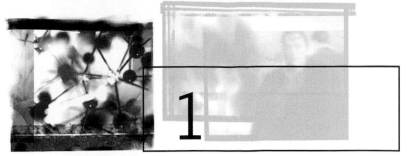

# 1 Human relationships

## 1.1 Introduction

From the moment that a human infant enters the world, the first of many relationships in their life begins, as over the following hours, days and years an enduring relationship forms between the infant and their caregiver. Indeed several psychological perspectives, including those of psychoanalysts and humanists, maintain that this first relationship is perhaps *the* most significant in shaping our psychological health and affecting our relationships with others for the rest of our lives. However, while our relationship with our parents may be one of the most influential, throughout our lives we will form countless others, including bonds with other members of our family, friendships with people at school and college, professional relationships with colleagues, and intimate relationships with those to whom we become very close.

## PRACTICAL Activity

Make a list of all of the various people with whom you have an ongoing relationship. This could include your parents, siblings, friends, people with whom you work, and more intimate acquaintances.

Next, write down the ways in which these relationships differ or are similar, such as the sort of things you might talk about with these people and the degree of trust you have in them.

This chapter will concentrate on the various aspects involved in human relationships and particularly those concerning our attraction toward other people. Beginning with the formation of our first relationship, we will then consider some of the factors that contribute towards interpersonal attraction, before looking at the ways in which psychologists have researched the concept of love. One of the facets of an intimate relationship between consenting adults is sexual behaviour and this too will be explored. Finally, since many long-term relationships undergo problems, sometimes resulting in breakdown, some of the factors that contribute towards this process will be considered.

# 1.2 Attraction, friendship and the development of relationships

From having completed the activity above you may have noticed that one way in which our varied relationships differs is in their degree of intimacy or closeness. Developing a sense of trust in others so that we are able and willing to confide in them is one hallmark of a friendship, but while very young children do not interact with others in this way initially, their trust in other people close to them does emerge at a very early age.

## Attachment and the need for intimacy

As mentioned earlier, the attachment process is regarded by many researchers as crucial for normal, healthy development in the child. Gradually during the first few months of life, the infant learns to distinguish between certain people in his or her surroundings, showing signs of contentment and pleasure when the caregiver is present, but distress when they are not. The consequences of the attachment bond being somehow disrupted have been well documented over the last 50 years, and you will be familiar with many of these studies from the Child Development module in *Advanced Psychology* (Pennington *et al.*, 2003). However, since we are concerned here with attachment in the context of human relationships, it is of particular interest to examine the age at which this early relationship is formed, as the following study highlights.

**Study 1.1**

**AIM** Schaffer and Callender (1959) conducted a study to examine the effects upon young children of a period of separation, and to identify the specific age at which infants become unduly upset by the absence of their caregiver.

**METHOD** In this particular case the separation was due to children having to go into hospital, and so an observational study was conducted on 76 infants aged between 3 and 51 weeks. The average duration of the infants' time spent in hospital was approximately two weeks and each participant was observed for the first few days of being admitted, and the last few days before going home. Various criteria were observed such as the frequency of crying, the amount of time spent playing with toys, and the infants' general responsiveness to other people. Furthermore, when the infants returned home, a further observation was conducted in order to examine any enduring effects the separation may have had.

**RESULT** The researchers noted that two distinct patterns of behaviour occurred, defined by the age of the infant. Specifically, infants aged around seven months or older were negatively affected by the separation from (in this case) their mother; for example, crying at her absence, being overly clingy when she visited, and being unwilling to interact with strangers. Furthermore, this state of anxiety continued when the infant returned home from hospital, as they often appeared highly insecure if left alone for any length of time. By contrast, infants younger than seven months showed no such symptoms and were largely left unscathed by the separation.

**CONCLUSION** Infants appear to form their first significant relationship from around seven months of age onwards, and from then on may be sensitive to this relationship being disrupted.

It follows from research such as this that if an infant has learned to differentiate between certain people by the middle half of their first year, then the investment of trust in that person also occurs at around the same time. This continues to develop in the child's other significant relationships outside of the family – their friendships. From studies of social cognition, and particularly children's friendships, researchers have noted a contrast in the way young children perceive desirable qualities in a friend. Berndt (1981) for example found that, in a sample of American children, it was only from around 10 or 11 years onwards that notions of trust and intimacy became important facets of their friendships. This was shown in the extent to which they were able to confide in their friend, compared with younger children who seemed to place more importance on superficial qualities such as how often they were telephoned by their friend.

Several parallels may also be drawn between relationships in childhood and adulthood, and some psychologists regard trust and intimacy to be among the main ingredients of adult friendships. For the post-Freudian Erikson, for example, being able to relate to another person in an intimate manner represented a key milestone in his psychosocial stage theory, and was highlighted as the major developmental task to successfully resolve in young adulthood (Erikson, 1963). Intimate relationships in adulthood have been found to involve three main processes: some form of emotional attachment between the two people, which may be characterised by feelings such as love; the meeting of certain psychological needs gained from caring for another person and sharing aspects of one's life with them; and interdependence between the two people such that each is reliant upon and influenced by the other (Brehm and Kassin, 1996).

Intimate relationships in adulthood are often accompanied by emotional feelings such as affection

## REFLECTIVE Activity

Psychologists studying the processes involved in intimacy in adulthood point out that relationships do not necessarily include all three of the features outlined above.

Consider some different adult relationships, such as an elderly couple who have been married for 50 years or a couple who have been dating for three weeks, and decide which of the three characteristics are likely to be present.

Undoubtedly, then, an intimate relationship provides considerable psychological benefits and may link in with other aspects of our personality. As with other facets of our personality, though, the need for intimacy is something in which individuals differ.

## PRACTICAL Activity

Working in small groups, construct a questionnaire to measure an individual's need for intimacy. You might begin by deciding what the main ingredients of intimacy are (closeness, trust, affection, etc.), and then decide on the format of the questionnaire.

You should also consider several other issues, including how the questions will be scored, the reliability and validity of the questionnaire, and any ethical aspects that should be addressed.

**Study 1.2**

**AIM** McAdams and Valliant (1982) were interested in how an individual's need for intimacy correlated with other aspects of their development.

**METHOD** A longitudinal study was conducted in which the researchers had 30-year-old males compose stories that were then scored in terms of references to intimacy, such as their need for commitment from another person. The participants were contacted again when they were 47 years old and the relationship between their intimacy scores (at 30) and their later psychological adjustment was measured.

**RESULT** A positive correlation was found between an individual's need for intimacy as a young adult and the extent to which they were considered 'well adjusted' in middle adulthood. Those whose stories had included several strong themes of intimacy were found to report greater satisfaction in their career and marriage.

**CONCLUSION** A high need for intimacy seems to be interwoven into our healthy psychological development, and a desire for commitment from another person, together with a wish to share feelings with them, seems to produce beneficial and enduring effects.

## Biological reasons for relationships

If, then, as we have seen, human beings are drawn to form relationships with others because it allows our needs to be met, and in addition promotes psychological health, this implies a common underlying reason. Furthermore if the forming of relationships is largely universal – that is, it is common to all cultures – then biological factors should underpin the process. The notion of being with others and seeking out their presence is known as affiliation and this process is closely tied to the forming of relationships. One way to appreciate its importance is to consider the consequences of being without any human company, and this was investigated in the study that follows.

**Study 1.3**

**AIM** Schachter (1959) was interested in how social isolation would affect individuals who were placed in an environment devoid of human company and, in particular, to see how long people could cope in such a setting.

**METHOD** Five paid male volunteers took part in the experiment and each person was placed individually in a specially designed room that contained only a bed, table, chair, lamp and toilet facilities. There were no windows in the room, and hence no natural daylight. Food and drink were left at the door at regular times, but the individual didn't see anyone, nor were they allowed books, a television or radio. Prior to entering the room each participant was told that they could leave the experiment at any time.

**RESULT** Of the five people that underwent the study, one of them had to leave after a period of only 20 minutes, while three more subjects each remained for two days. However, while two of them appeared relatively unaffected by the experience, one said that they would never repeat it and had felt unsettled throughout. The fifth participant remained for eight days and later reported that while they had felt uneasy during their stay in the room they did not appear to have suffered any serious effects.

**CONCLUSION** It would appear that, for most people, a period of social isolation and zero contact with 'the outside world' is extremely difficult to deal with as we seem to need to be with others. However, there are individual differences in the extent to which people are able to tolerate such circumstances.

## EVALUATIVE COMMENT

**Although many of us would find it difficult to deal with the surroundings in which the subjects in this study found themselves, there are moments for each of us when we greatly value being alone. While this study presents an interesting test of human beings' need for affiliation and social interaction it does not readily generalise to the wider population since it only involved five participants. Furthermore, the participants were paid volunteers, which also highlights questions concerning its generalisation, and in addition introduces the possibility that demand characteristics could have influenced the outcome. Even with the small sample tested we are reminded that individual differences play an important role; various studies have stressed the value of spending time in isolation from other human beings. Suedfeld (1982) suggests that for some people isolation can be very exhilarating, being actively sought by artists and explorers, while for others it can provide a deep and meaningful religious experience. Undoubtedly periods of social isolation may be spiritually rewarding for some as long as these are freely chosen and desirable.**

One of the major contributions towards biological reasons for relationships comes from the area of sociobiology, which essentially focuses upon the role of biology in social behaviour. More specifically within this field is a branch sometimes referred to as evolutionary social psychology, which is based upon the theories of Charles Darwin, whose contribution to psychology you may recall from your previous studies. From a Darwinian perspective the continuity of the species is dependent upon reproductive success and so intimate relationships, and in particular mating, could be seen as a means of ensuring survival of the human race. According to this approach, for men, a woman's physical appearance is a priority, whereas women consider a man's resources more important than looks since this signals a partner who would be better able to provide for any offspring. Several studies seem to confirm this view. For example, Buss and Schmitt (1993) argued that based on an evolutionary approach, men should be more interested in the physical appearance of women, a factor possibly indicating something of their reproductive ability. They questioned around 10 000 adults in 37 countries worldwide about the relative importance of a variety of features in determining a suitable spouse, and found that women preferred men who were hard-working, ambitious and with a high earning potential, while men, in comparison, placed physical attractiveness and appearance at the top of their list of desirable qualities.

Further differences in male and female priorities were investigated in a study by Clark and Hatfield (1989), who had confederates ask opposite-sex students one of three questions: whether they would go out with them that evening, whether they would come back with them to their flat, or whether they would go to bed with them. When female students were approached by a male confederate, approximately 50 per cent agreed to the first question, around 3 per cent to the second question but none to the last question. By contrast, when male students were asked the same questions by a female stooge, 50 per cent agreed to a date, 70 per cent to return to the woman's apartment, and over 70 per cent were willing to go to bed with her.

## REFLECTIVE Activity

While studies such as the one above provide a useful source of information on the different aspects of male and female priorities from a 'relationship', they also raise several issues found with research of this kind.

Read through this study again and list any problems with the design of the study as well as any ethical considerations. What other factors might explain the considerable differences noted between the answers given by the males and females?

The evolutionary approach to relationships provides an interesting interpretation for the biological roots of relationship formation, although it appears to be limited in its scope to traditional heterosexual relationships. Furthermore, in addition to the biological 'drives' that lead us to affiliate with other people, social and cultural factors are also important in the attraction process. 'Attractiveness', for instance, is a concept that differs in many other cultures, which implies a strong contribution of learning and experience. However, social psychologists have identified several factors that many researchers agree are influential in relationship formation and interpersonal attraction, and these will be considered next.

## Factors affecting interpersonal attraction

As you walk around the town in which you live, you may occasionally bump into people whom you know, and as you approach the road in which you live the likelihood is that you will be familiar with many more people. Other than the members of our family and our relatives everyone else now known to us was, at one time, a complete stranger. How, then, did we become an acquaintance, friend or someone even closer to those individuals in our social circle?

Aronson (1999) gives four reasons for why we like other people, and says that we particularly like those:

- who have interests and beliefs that are similar to our own
- who have the same kinds of skills or abilities that we possess
- who have personality characteristics that we find appealing, such as kindness and honesty
- who like us.

Although under certain circumstances a relationship may become intimate in a very short time, usually relationships develop gradually and progress from initial contact to discovering a more solid basis for friendship, such as having certain things in common. Researchers acknowledge that many relationships often start from people having frequent or regular contact, and this factor will be looked at first.

### PROXIMITY

This term refers to our nearness or closeness to others, and it may be considered as providing the initial means for social interaction to occur. Sometimes known as propinquity, it essentially suggests that we are more likely to form friendships with those who are physically or geographically near to us. Festinger *et al.* (1950) investigated the development of friendship among married students in a university hall of residence and noted that 41 per cent of couples were more friendly with those who lived in adjacent rooms and then with those living just a few doors away. Furthermore, only 10 per cent of the married couples had made friends with people who lived at the end of the hall corridor. However, proximity alone cannot guarantee friendship. While the students in this study support the idea that frequent contact with others and hence familiarity often leads us to like them, it could also highlight undesirable qualities in their behaviour. Thus while there is a very good chance that you are on friendly terms with your next-door neighbour, there is also a possibility that your increased familiarity with them has led to a dislike of them.

## PRACTICAL Activity

One way in which social interactions may be measured (a term known as sociometry) is by using sociograms. For example, imagine watching members of a sports team interacting with each other during a match. It would be possible, using observational skills, to determine which people had more contact with their fellow team members than others, by, for instance, counting the number of times they received passes of the ball. This idea may, with a little adaptation, be applied to your circle of friends or the people in your street.

Draw up a simple plan of the houses in your street, and then indicate with arrows the direction and number in which interactions occur from your house to and from those of your neighbours and other houses.

## PHYSICAL ATTRACTIVENESS

Aside from living near to someone, the factor that seems more than any other to affect interpersonal attraction is the extent to which we find other people attractive. In addition, strong stereotypes exist in connection with those whom we consider good-looking. For example, Dion *et al.* (1972) found that their participants rated attractive individuals as having more socially desirable qualities and that, furthermore, it was expected that these people would be more likely to experience greater success in their lives in the future than those people considered unattractive. As well as having different expectations about physically attractive individuals, our thoughts and judgements about them also appear to differ. Sigall and Ostrove (1973), for instance, found that participants gave more lenient prison sentences to an attractive female described in a 'criminal case account' as having committed a burglary. More interestingly, perhaps, when her 'crime' was seen as being related to her attractiveness (a description was given of how the woman had swindled a man out of his money) she was given a much more severe sentence.

As mentioned earlier, from a biological viewpoint, men tend to be more influenced by the attractiveness of their potential partner, but several studies have found that, certainly in terms of dating, attractiveness appears important to both people. Walster *et al.* (1966) randomly matched new university students after they had initially completed a personality test and set them up with a 'blind date' at a student social event. Each of the couples was later given a questionnaire and this indicated that the overwhelming factor determining whether couples liked each other and wished to see the other person again, was physical attractiveness.

Attractiveness, then, seems to make people instantly appealing, but often this characteristic becomes less important as the relationship progresses. While couples that have been together for many years will report that they still find their partner physically attractive, the relationship is usually more likely to flourish as individuals discover other features about their companion.

## SIMILARITY

While the extent to which we consider another person physically attractive may often provide a starting point for a relationship, another basis for the development of friendships is shared interests and similar attitudes. If you think for a moment about the people who are close to you, including same-sex friends, you may appreciate that you have many things in common, such as an interest in the same type of music, sport or even political issues.

## PRACTICAL Activity

Apart from interests and attitudes, individuals can resemble each other on many other dimensions. Make a list of the various characteristics you share with your friends.

You might also consider if you differ in certain ways, and whether or not this is an obstacle to your friendship.

From attempting the activity above you may have identified several ways in which we are

Physical attractiveness is an important factor in the process of interpersonal attraction

similar to our friends. Brehm and Kassin (1996) highlight a number of these features, which include demographic characteristics such as age, ethnic group, educational level and socioeconomic status, as well as personality and mood. The link between such factors and interpersonal attraction was demonstrated in a study by Newcomb (1961), who studied a large sample of college students in their hall of residence, and found that liking tended to increase the more similar individuals were on a variety of demographic factors such as those listed above.

## EVALUATIVE COMMENT

**Much of the research described so far has been conducted on samples of university students; as such, these are usually opportunity samples gathered for the study principally out of convenience. In addition, students are often paid for their participation in the research, and so these aspects raise questions over the generalisation of the findings. Another methodological issue is that some of the findings are based upon correlational data, and so causal factors are not clearly evident. Another problem with research in this area is the difficulty of separating out the influential factors, since similarity, for example, cannot be examined in complete isolation from physical attractiveness.**

Our attraction to those with similar characteristics, interests or attitudes to ourselves may help to confirm our own values since, in a way, a person who enjoys the same kind of food or music may actually help to promote our self-confidence, as they reinforce our own belief system. However, there are exceptions to this explanation as sometimes relationships can prosper for many years where considerable dissimilarities exist between couples. Instead of similarity, complementarity can sometimes provide harmony between two people where, for example, someone with a loud, outgoing personality finds a quiet, introverted person attractive. In keeping with Heider's balance theory (1958), which emphasises the role of consistency within interpersonal relationships, another factor emerges that affects our liking of others: whether or not the feeling is mutual.

### RECIPROCAL LIKING

Although it may seem fairly obvious, the basis for reciprocal liking is quite simple: we tend to like those who like us. This is even apparent at a physiological level, as Hess (1975) found. He presented male students with what appeared to be two identical photographs of an attractive young woman. The participants were simply asked to indicate which photograph they preferred. Although the results yielded a significant difference in the choice made, interestingly subjects admitted being unable to give a specific reason. In fact the picture that was most frequently selected as the more attractive of the two had been very slightly altered so that the pupils appeared larger. This involuntary action of pupil dilation occurs when we are presented with a pleasing image, and so essentially the participants were showing a liking for someone who liked them in return.

In effect we are receiving positive feedback from those who signal a liking for us, and this may serve to increase our self-esteem, thereby giving us a psychological boost. Walster (1965) looked at the interaction between self-esteem and attraction in a study where female students were invited to take part in a psychology experiment. Whilst waiting in a room for the study to commence, the women were approached individually by an attractive male confederate who, after talking to them for a while, asked them for a date. During the experiment that followed, the participants' self-esteem was manipulated by the researcher, who gave them either positive or negative feedback from a number of tests they had taken. Following this, the participants were asked to rate several people whom they knew, one of which included the male they had spoken to in the waiting room earlier. The results showed that females who were given negative feedback rated the confederate higher than those who received positive feedback. This suggests that their lowered self-esteem had led them to express more liking for a person who liked them, thereby raising their confidence.

# REFLECTIVE Activity

Make a list of ethical issues that apply to investigations of human behaviour, and then read over the study outlined above again and highlight the ethical issues specific to this study. You may like to consult the ethical guidelines from a professional body such as the American Psychological Association (APA, 2002) to assist you in this. Next, consider how these issues should have been dealt with in this particular study.

# 1.3 Need for intimacy and the development of relationships

The presence of the factors covered in the section above would seem to increase the likelihood that two people will form a relationship, but they do not guarantee that the relationship will endure over time. Human relationships are often complex interactions of many criteria and as such their development has attracted the interest of psychologists who have proposed both theories and stages to account for the ways in which they unfold.

## Theories of relationship development

Several theories of relationship development have been proposed, based on psychological principles that the reader will already have encountered (see Pennington *et al.*, 2002). Indeed, earlier in this chapter one of the biological reasons for relationships – namely the evolutionary perspective – may be applied here. Theorists of this persuasion argue that males and females entered into a more complex social arrangement approximately one million years ago, when a hunter-gatherer lifestyle began to emerge in which males embarked upon hunting expeditions in order to provide for their mates, offspring and selves. According to this view the development of more enduring relationships would have provided a motive for the males' return and ultimately helped these 'new' societies to thrive (Gleitman *et al.*, 1999).

An alternative to the evolutionary approach is the economic model that is represented in social exchange theory (Homans, 1961). Here individuals are perceived as entering into relationships on the basis of the relative gains or losses associated with them, and this principle applies whether the person is a work colleague or potential spouse.

# PRACTICAL Activity

Consider several different relationships that people may have with others and then, using social exchange theory, write the heading 'rewards' and 'costs' at the top of a sheet of paper. List all of the rewards and costs that come to mind for each of the relationships. You could also try this activity for any personal relationships you may have as well as relationships that have been discontinued. Notice whether or not the rewards outweigh the costs, since the model would predict that we would stay in the relationship only if this was the case.

When specifically applied to intimate relationships, research suggests that the proportion of rewards to costs can determine the duration of the relationship, at least in the early stages. Furthermore, most intimate relationships do not seem to encounter detrimental problems (costs) at the beginning, as the pair are in the throes of excitement that the new venture brings. Rusbult (1983) estimated that approximately 12 weeks into a relationship 'costs' were starting to affect the satisfaction that the couple had about their partnership. Several elements have been proposed in social exchange theory, particularly in terms of the expectations that individuals have as they enter into a relationship. One of these, according to Kelley (1983), is the investment that each person commits to the partnership. This essentially refers to the resources (such as time) that individuals are prepared to put in to the friendship to try to ensure the relationship succeeds. In a way this represents a form of psychological commitment and is important since, if it fails, their 'investment' is lost; the mental and physical effort contributed to the partnership cannot be retrieved. In this way the rewards of a satisfying and meaningful relationship far outweigh any costs incurred through devoting mental and physical energy to the process.

The final theory to be considered here is balance theory (Heider, 1958), briefly referred to earlier in connection with the role of reciprocity in attraction. As a theory of relationship development it proposes that individuals seek consistency (or balance) in their relationships with others and that, furthermore, any sources of imbalance render the person in an uncomfortable psychological state that they are motivated to avoid. At a simple level, if Tahir likes Holly but Holly dislikes Tahir, then a relationship between the two is unlikely to prosper. Within this model, relationship formation and development is usually illustrated by an interaction between three people (or two people and an attitude object), and this enables the distinction between balanced and unbalanced combinations to become apparent. This is illustrated in the examples shown in Figures 1.3 and 1.4.

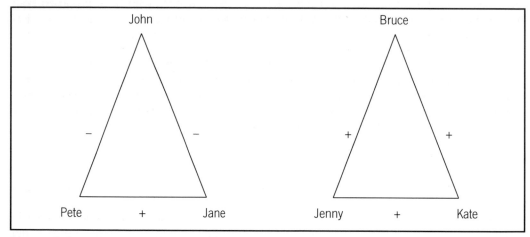

Figure 1.3: Balanced combinations

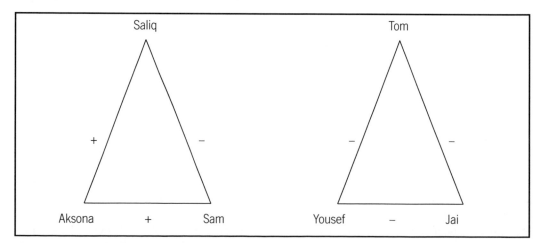

Figure 1.4: Unbalanced combinations

Figure 1.3 represents two balanced relationships. In the first case a potential relationship may be seen between Pete and Jane, since Pete likes Jane, for instance, and both of them dislike John. In the second example, once again there is consistency between a group of three friends who each like each other. Figure 1.4, however, demonstrates unbalanced states, and as such the relationships denote inconsistency in the sense that they are either unworkable or perhaps threatened by breakdown. First, the relationship between Aksona and Saliq is tenuous and possibly strained by their contrasting feelings for Sam. In the second scenario, a relationship cannot arise because each person dislikes the other. Thus in both of these cases the model would predict that in order for consistency to occur one or more of the people concerned would have to alter their feelings for the others in their triad. For example, Saliq may learn to like Sam, which in turn could strengthen his relationship with Aksona.

## EVALUATIVE COMMENT

**Despite the ways in which these theories may usefully be applied to describe and explain the development of relationships, there are limitations to each. Evolutionary theory, for instance, has biological roots and as such implies that much of our behaviour within relationships follows a natural 'order', thereby ignoring to a large extent the role of learning, as well as cognitive processes. Hill (1998) points out that models such as that offered by social exchange theory are largely based on the beliefs and values of capitalist cultures where greater emphasis is placed upon gains and losses, rewards and costs (albeit in an economic sense). Furthermore, this approach implies that such motives are at the core of our choices and decisions within relationships, which is a rather cold, calculating interpretation that would seem to discount genuine love and affection. Finally, balance theory, centred upon three individuals, is literally restricted by the number of people involved in any given interaction, and the differences in the strength of feeling that A, for example, has for B rather than C, are not quantified, since liking (or disliking) are assumed to be uniform (Hill, 1998).**

## Stages in relationship development

A stage theory of development usually meets several criteria: progression through the stages follows an orderly sequence and there are qualitative differences apparent at each stage. Numerous psychological approaches have proposed this kind of sequential development, including the work of Freud and Erikson, as well as the theory of cognitive growth in children offered by Piaget. As far as relationships are concerned, we have already suggested that, initially, our friends and more intimate acquaintances were once strangers to us, and such a shift can be envisaged to occur over a period of time that involves changes in how we view the other person. A simple model of this progression can be seen in Figure 1.5.

Figure 1.5: Stages in relationship development

According to this view the process of relationship formation and development begins when we simply become aware of the other person's presence, such as when we first notice a colleague at work. This may be influenced by one or more of the factors discussed above, such as physical attractiveness. The next stage involves making some sort of contact with the person, which may range from having a polite conversation to asking them out on a date. The third process, self-disclosure, involves a significant leap in terms of how much trust we place in the other person, and will be examined in more detail later. Although this is a rather basic model it nevertheless adheres to the characteristics of a stage theory in presenting a series of steps that relationships follow. However, it gives no indication of the time spent at each stage, a feature that was remedied in a more detailed theory presented by Murstein (1987). This model also comprises three stages and is known as the stimulus–value–role theory. In the first stage greater importance is given to external stimuli such as physical attractiveness, often found when we meet a person for the first time. Following continued interactions with a person (approximately two to seven meetings, according to Murstein) we then shift away from attributes such as a person's looks as being the most important factor, and focus instead upon the ways in which our attitudes and values share a similarity. In the third stage (eight meetings or more) prominence is placed upon the extent to which the person with whom we are having a relationship meets the criteria that we might deem necessary for long-term commitment. Here our expectations of the roles for each person in the relationship take precedence.

The notion of stages in relationship development is appealing, but here as with many other stage theories in psychology, one of the main flaws concerns the extent to which such models may be universally applied. The wide variety of intimate relationships that is found presents difficulties when gauged against such orderly and constrained sequences. For example, consider the differences between a couple who never move on to a relationship involving commitment to each other, even after many years, in comparison with one where the couple fall in love at the first meeting. In addition, social and cultural factors play an important role, as with couples brought together in arranged marriages, who often grow to love each other. Before investigating the concept of love within intimate relationships in more detail, another facet of behaviour that although common to all intimate relationships shows enormous variation will be outlined: self-disclosure.

## REFLECTIVE Activity

Consider how you might attempt to test the stage theories outlined above. What research method or methods might be employed? If, for example, a questionnaire is seen as the most appropriate method, who would be the most suitable participants? Discuss these and any other relevant questions in groups, and remember especially that such an exercise is fraught with ethical issues.

## Factors affecting self-disclosure

When we have spent time with a person that we like and a relationship with them is developing, one way in which this may become evident is the extent to which we reveal personal information about our self to them. This is called self-disclosure and marks an important landmark in the step towards getting to know and trust someone, whether it is a friend or more intimate acquaintance. When is it appropriate to disclose information to another, though, and what form should this information take? Altman and Taylor (1973) proposed the theory of social penetration, which suggests that in the early phase of getting to know someone the information we talk about is rather superficial and we are likely to discuss quite neutral topics such as the worsening weather. Gradually, though, as our feelings about the other person grow, we tend to feel able to share more private, intimate issues with them. Thus we may discuss quite personal health problems or our concerns regarding relationships with other individuals that are close to us.

Furthermore, research indicates that this process is often based on a reciprocal exchange of information in that there is a tendency, at least in the early stages of a relationship, to match the level of disclosure that the other individual presents to us. For example, it would be deemed quite inappropriate to expose our innermost values or worries to a relative stranger. Self-disclosure, then, requires careful monitoring as the relationship is forming, in order that the person whom we like does not perceive us as either too aloof or too forthcoming. Despite these common underlying 'rules' governing the exchange of information about ourselves to others, individual differences do occur, and in this regard psychologists have focused on gender.

**Study 1.4**

**AIM** Dindia and Allen (1992) were interested in gender differences in self-disclosure among same-sex and opposite-sex gender groups.

**METHOD** They carried out a meta-analysis (a research method that analyses a large number of data or findings gathered from other studies) on over 200 studies of self-disclosure in the USA, totalling almost 24 000 participants.

**RESULT** Of the two genders women were found to disclose more information than men, and in particular, women were more likely to place their confidence in other women as people to reveal personal information to. Although men did tend to disclose information about themselves to both other men and to women, it appeared they were more comfortable self-disclosing to other men than to women.

**CONCLUSION** Males and females do not show self-disclosure to the same extent and one of the main factors involved in the process appears to be not only the gender of the discloser but also the gender of the individual to whom the information is imparted.

Further research into same-sex friendships has pointed out the possible influence of social and cultural factors. Wright (1982), for example, suggested that women's interactions with each other tend to be at a 'face-to-face' level, such that women will converse in close proximity directly facing each other. Men on the other hand are described as preferring a 'side-by-side' posture when they relate to each other. For example, two male friends might go to see a football match together. Interestingly these findings tend to correspond to work conducted on personal space – the invisible zone around each of us that we guard from intrusion by strangers. Fisher and Byrne (1975) had male or female confederates sit next to people working in a library. When the confederate sat directly opposite a male student the individual showed signs of discomfort and placed books or other obstacles between them, whereas they did not appear concerned when they took up a seat at the side of them. With female students they tended to experience more discomfort when the confederate sat adjacent to them, appearing at ease in a 'face-to-face' arrangement (see Figure 1.6). Applied to self-disclosure we may speculate that women are better able to relate to each other on an emotional level, and that this kind of intimacy is facilitated by facing the other person. You may also recall that Gilligan's work on moral reasoning (Gilligan, 1982) suggests that young women tend to favour a more caring and connecting perspective as their basis for dealing with moral decisions, all of which perhaps implies an underlying difference between the genders on a range of issues, including that of self-disclosure.

It is worth noting, though, that there are exceptions to these findings on same-sex friendships in self-disclosure. There are circumstances,

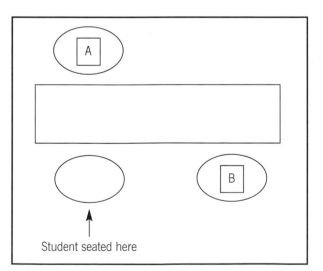

Figure 1.6: Gender differences in personal space (adapted from Fisher and Byrne, 1975); males showed discomfort when a confederate was seated at position A, whereas females tended to be more ill at ease if they were seated at position B

for instance, where men can attain emotionally close relationships with other men to the extent that they disclose information to each other in much the same way that women might. Another aspect that seems to affect self-disclosure is a person's sexual orientation, particularly since this appears to contradict the gender differences discussed so far. Factors that play a role in determining sexual orientation will be looked at in due course, but next we will examine the contribution that psychologists have made towards increasing our understanding of an emotional state that may be fundamental to intimate relationships – love.

## 1.4 Love and marriage

So far this chapter has considered the various processes that attract us to others, and although much of the research on human relationships is applicable to both opposite and same-sex friendships, as has been shown above regarding self-disclosure, one major distinction involves the difference between liking and loving. At what point does liking develop into loving? Research in this area has attempted to clarify this question by employing a variety of methods, including the development of scales to 'measure' love. In addition, psychologists working in this field have proposed that love takes many forms, some of which will now be considered.

### Explanations of love

One of the first attempts to devise a means of measuring the differences between those whom we like and those whom we love was put forward by Rubin (1970). He argued that loving compared to liking involved a qualitatively different set of feelings, and he constructed a scale that required respondents to rate their friends and then those with whom they were romantically involved. In one study he gave out the Liking and Loving Scales to college students who were 'dating steadily' and later observed them via a one-way mirror. Those who had obtained a high score on the scale gazed into each other's eyes more often compared with those couples that had achieved a low score (Rubin, 1973).

Other researchers have gone on to refine and categorise love into distinct types. Hatfield (1988), for example, identified passionate (romantic) love and companionate love. The first of these evokes a strong emotional response and the person may experience high levels of arousal accompanied with an intense attraction for the target of their love. The Passionate Love Scale (Hatfield and Rapson, 1987) allows a person to direct their thoughts and feelings about a specific loved one, by requiring them to indicate their agreement to several statements that cover the range of characteristics associated with passionate love. For example, 'I would rather be with _____ than anyone else.' The second form of love is companionate love, and although it may contain elements of passionate love in that there may be a strong attraction and attachment between the couple, the main ingredients tend to be a sense of devoted loyalty, respect and trust in the significant other. In a sense, the two are close friends as well as lovers. It is possible to conceive of this type of love as more common to long-term relationships where perhaps the initial intensity has subsided, although many relationships do not fit neatly into this stereotype.

### The triangular theory of love

In a more comprehensive approach to this subject, Sternberg (1986) devised the triangular theory of love, which in addition to identifying discrete types of love, looks at the ways in which they interact, and in so doing create a wide variety of different forms.

As the name suggests, Sternberg's model is based around three main types of love: passion, intimacy and commitment. Passion may be seen as a driving force and in many ways resembles the conception of passionate love described above, since it involves romantic elements and intense sexual attraction. Intimacy reflects the emotions and feelings felt by each of the people that keep them close, while commitment is represented by underlying thoughts and beliefs, and an intention from both parties to maintain the stability of the relationship. What separates Sternberg's theory from other conceptions of love, though, is the variety of combinations that are possible, each of which has its own features. For instance, if each of the three main elements is present then a state of consummate love is found, where the couple have all of the ingredients of love in equal measure. Conversely, different forms of love are found where one or more of

Romantic or companionate love?

the three components are absent. These are summarised in Figure 1.8 on page 16.

In this diagram the three main elements are represented as building blocks, and the end product is shown in the right-hand column. Having a complete 'set' results in consummate love, but if one or more blocks are missing then the type of love experienced is changed accordingly. For example, if two people have intimacy and commitment within their relationship but it lacks passion, then they experience companionate love.

## Styles of love

In many respects similar to the triangular theory in that they cover a wide variety of types and permit combinations of love to be formed, two other models will now be outlined briefly. Lee (1988) conceptualised love in terms of colours based on an ancient Greek typology, which produced six individual styles. His results were gained from conducting a large-scale survey from which different patterns of love emerged:

- Eros (romantic love)
- Agape (altruistic, selfless love)
- Ludus (playful, flirtatious love)
- Mania (possessive, obsessive love)
- Storge (companionate love)
- Pragma (practical love).

This work was followed up by Hendrick and Hendrick (1995), who researched the different combinations that the primary styles, or colours (Eros, Ludus, Storge), produced. Secondary styles were gained from combining two of the primary styles so that Storge and Eros together gave Agape; Eros and Ludus, Mania; and Ludus and Storge, Pragma. Hendrick and Hendrick (1995) found that there were gender differences in these styles, with males tending to seek a playful, emotional experience in their loving relationship, while females prioritised friendship and more practical aspects in love, such as seeking someone who meets certain requirements and is able to provide for them. You may have noticed that these findings would appear to be

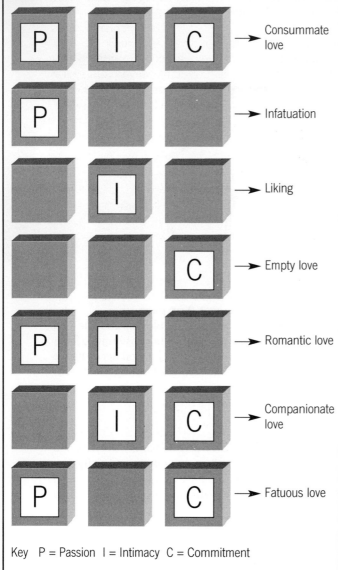

Key   P = Passion   I = Intimacy   C = Commitment

Figure 1.8: Possible combinations in the triangular theory of love (adapted from Sternberg, 1986)

consistent with the evolutionary approach to relationship formation discussed earlier, where males and females differ principally in terms of what they expect from a potential partner.

## REFLECTIVE Activity

Look back over this section on the various types and styles of love, and make a list of the similarities and differences between each approach or type. In small groups discuss the strengths and weaknesses of the various explanations and theories of love that have been described.

## 1.5 Sex and sexual relationships

From an evolutionary point of view, mating can be regarded chiefly as a means of ensuring the continuation of the species. However, sexual behaviour is of course much more than this; it enables couples within intimate relationships to experience not only a physical closeness, but also in many ways, to strengthen the emotional bond that exists between them. This section will consider several issues that are pertinent to intimate relationships, beginning with factors that affect our choice of sexual partner.

### Sexual orientation

The vast majority of people are heterosexual, a term derived from the Greek word 'heteros' meaning 'other', and are sexually attracted to individuals of the opposite sex. Some people, however, are sexually attracted to those of the same sex, a term referred to as homosexuality (from the Greek 'homos' meaning 'same'). Although the expression is used to describe both males attracted to other males and females attracted to other females, the latter are usually known as lesbians. The last few decades have witnessed a greater awareness of homosexuality, and people's prejudices about the 'gay community' are gradually declining. In addition to these two forms of sexuality are bisexuals ('bi-' meaning 'two'), which is a word used to define those who are sexually attracted to both males and females.

At this point it is also worth mentioning two other terms that are frequently confused with an individual's sexual orientation. Transvestism is a label used to describe those who obtain sexual gratification from dressing in the clothes of the opposite sex, and is usually, but not exclusively, applied to males who achieve sexual pleasure by dressing in women's clothing. This form of behaviour, though, is frequently unrelated to sexual orientation such that a male transvestite is otherwise heterosexual in his choice of sexual partner. Transsexualism, on the other hand, refers to a condition where people believe that they are the 'wrong' sex, and transsexuals will often report a feeling of being trapped in the wrong body. Several notable cases of this condition have come to light in recent years where individuals have undergone corrective surgery to reassign their gender. In this case, sexual orientation is a central issue since a male transsexual, for example, desires to become female and then in this role enjoy intimate relations with a male. This, then, is quite different from homosexuality.

## PRACTICAL Activity

Design a questionnaire to measure people's sexual attitudes. You should consider several relevant issues such as the sampling method and target population as well as the format of the questionnaire. Once the scale has been constructed, conduct a pilot study before administering the questions to the main sample. You should also assess the ethical issues and implications of investigating this area of human relationships, and consider ways in which the reliability and validity of the questionnaire could be monitored.

## HIV transmission

It has been estimated by the United Nations that approximately 8000 people die every day from HIV/AIDS (Crawford, 2002). HIV (human immunodeficiency virus) is the infective agent that causes AIDS (acquired immune deficiency syndrome), and since it first began to appear in news headlines 20 or so years ago, it has had an enormous impact on patterns of sexual behaviour. The virus can be passed via bodily fluids, and because of this the two groups of people most at risk of being infected are those who practise 'unsafe' sex and those who inject drugs intravenously.

Initially, the AIDS epidemic of the 1980s seemed to spread throughout the male homosexual community and this gave rise to a reinforcement of negative feelings towards this section of the population. However, many people, particularly from westernised cultures, have become better educated in terms of both the risks and preventative action. Elsewhere, in developing countries, the statistics show an alarming growth in the spread of the virus, with more than 28 million Africans presently infected (Crawford, 2002).

Educational programmes provide one method of informing people of effective strategies to reduce the risk of becoming infected by the virus. The practice of safe sex (using a condom) is paramount, as is the need to be certain of an intending partner's sexual history. However, the relationship between attitudes and behaviour is generally

**Try another one?**

HIV awareness poster from the Terence Higgins Trust

inconsistent as has been well documented (see Pennington *et al.*, 2002). There is a need for further research and education schemes where school-age people are targeted, and psychologists have much to offer in this respect. At a recent conference, the contribution that professionals could make to the AIDS epidemic was highlighted:

> **HIV needs psychology … research is essential in the areas of prevention, adherence, stigma and removing policy barriers to prevention and care … as well as in areas such as gender inequality and homophobia, as these are the driving causes of the epidemic.**
>
> **(Coates, cited in Crawford, 2002)**

## Psychosexual behaviour

Attitudes and behaviour towards sex and sexuality have changed tremendously over the past 50 or so years. Earlier still, during the reign of Queen Victoria (1837–1901), sex was an absolutely private matter that was never even referred to in public, and sexual behaviour outside of marriage was largely regarded as intolerable. It was within this climate of opinion that Freud (1856–1939) developed his psychosexual theory of human behaviour, which even today challenges the ways in which human relationships are perceived.

However, it was not until the late 1930s that human sexuality was first thoroughly researched when Kinsey *et al.* produced what became known as the Kinsey Report (see the following Study).

**Study 1.5**

**AIM** Kinsey, Pomeroy and Martin (1948) were interested in finding out the scope of sexual attitudes and behaviour of adults in the USA.

**METHOD** Approximately 18 000 volunteers were interviewed by a trained team of researchers on a range of issues related to their sexual behaviour and activity, such as masturbation, heterosexual and homosexual experiences. Ethical issues were fully accounted for and special codes used to mask individual identities and thus ensure confidentiality. Participants had the right to refuse to answer any questions on matters they did not wish to disclose.

**RESULT** Among the findings several notable features emerged: sexual activity appeared closely related to age, with males, for example, peaking at around 30 years of age; approximately 92 per cent of the males in the sample had at some time masturbated compared with 58 per cent of the females; figures for premarital sex revealed a more permissive attitude than might have been envisaged in the 1940s with around 50 per cent of the females having had intercourse before marriage.

**CONCLUSION** Generally, sexual attitudes and behaviour were more informed than may have been expected, and overall the survey revealed considerable variation and individual differences.

The findings from the Kinsey Report present a detailed picture of the nature of human sexuality, although caution must be exercised before attempting to generalise the findings. For example, all of the respondents were volunteers and the study is now more than 50 years old, which raises problems when making comparisons to present-day views. In addition, it is culture-specific in that it relates largely to western ideals, and the sexual attitudes and behaviour of other cultures are based around a different set of values.

Since this survey, and particularly the sexual revolution of the 1960s, there has been a move towards a more open discussion of sexual issues. The widely held stereotype of sex as a predominant topic of interest solely for males is gradually being dispelled, and the last 10 or 20 years have witnessed a huge increase in magazines and literature targeting women of all ages in which sexual matters are regularly featured. Despite this trend, research still points to differences in males' and females' expectations regarding sexual relationships. Generally, it is suggested, women desire emotional closeness and commitment within a sexual relationship, while men are more likely to indulge in casual sex, although again this varies as many females adopt a promiscuous lifestyle (Hatfield *et al.*, 1989). These individual differences were highlighted in work by Simpson and Gangestad (1991) in which they investigated issues such as the need for love in a sexual relationship, in a measure known as the sociosexual orientation inventory. The authors proposed a continuum of sociosexuality that attempts to classify men and women according to their attitudes and behaviour (see Figure 1.10).

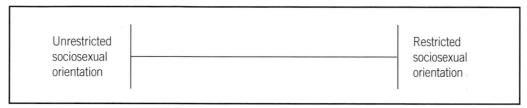

**Figure 1.10:** Extreme 'types' of sociosexuality (adapted from Simpson and Gangestad, 1991)

## REFLECTIVE Activity

This inventory acknowledges that both males and females can fit into either category (or somewhere in between) according to their sociosexual orientation, and therefore challenges the notion that men fall into one group while women occupy the other.

Write the headings 'restricted' and 'unrestricted' on a sheet of paper, and list the attitudes and behaviours that you would expect people to hold who fell into either of these categories.

Consider the strengths and weaknesses of the sociosexual orientation inventory.

### Nature-nurture debate in relation to sexual orientation

So far we have seen that sexual relationships are influenced by several factors, such as emotional involvement and the need for intimacy, but underlying each of these aspects is the basic attraction that we have for others that defines our sexual orientation. Central to this is the extent to which our sexual preferences are determined by our genes or the environment in which we learn and are raised. Just as the influence of hormones (at around four to eight weeks in the developing embryo) is thought to be critical in determining the gender of the offspring (Money and Ehrhardt, 1972), so too, some researchers believe, the endocrine system plays a role in determining sexual orientation, and in particular homosexuality. Animal studies using rats have found, for instance, that stress during pregnancy may be a factor, and that as a result of stressors the level of sex hormone production is influenced, which in turn affects the sexual development of male pups (Anderson *et al.*, 1986). However, with studies of animals such as this, care must be taken when interpreting the findings, particularly with the issue of generalisation. One line of thought, though, was that male homosexuals possessed lower levels of sex hormone, but Kinsey *et al.* (1948), in their study of human sexuality, noted that boosting the levels of androgens (sex hormones produced, for example, by the testes in males) increased sexual appetite but did not in any way alter the sexual preferences of the recipient of the treatment.

Other research into a biologically determined cause pursued a different line of enquiry. LeVay (1991), for instance, studied the brain structures of deceased male heterosexuals and homosexuals, and noticed that a region of the hypothalamus was enlarged in the homosexual corpses. While this observation does not provide conclusive evidence that a specific brain structure is directly involved in setting a person's sexual orientation, it hints at possible prenatal influences when the brain is still undergoing development (Carlson, 1993).

**Study 1.6**

**AIM** Bell, Weinberg and Hammersmith (1981) were interested in identifying the factors that influenced sexual preference among male and female homosexuals.

**METHOD** Between 1969 and 1970, approximately 1000 lesbians and gay men were interviewed from in and around the San Francisco area of the United States. The participants were recruited from those who responded to newspaper advertisements as well as from venues popular with members of San Francisco's large gay community. In addition to questions concerning their sexual behaviour, the respondents were also asked about their past and present relationships with members of their family, together with childhood experiences.

**RESULT** Although the findings did not reveal one distinct explanation, several contributing factors appeared to be significant, among which were: identification with parents, early sexual encounters, and gender roles in childhood. On these points, it appeared that the participants' sexual preferences were not influenced by the extent to which they identified with the opposite-sex parent as a child, nor did the participants report being more likely (than heterosexuals) to have had a first sexual experience with someone of the same sex. However, gender nonconformity in childhood was significantly related to sexual orientation in both the males and females that were interviewed. A major factor also seemed to be that respondents experienced 'sexual feelings' some years prior to homosexual behaviour.

**CONCLUSION** Sexual preference may be brought about to some extent by biological influences, as the participants seemed to 'resist' cultural and social factors. These influences may set the way that gender and sexual development occurs.

A greater emphasis was placed on the contribution of environmental factors by Freud's psychoanalytical theory. Freud (1930) considered all people to be inherently bisexual, but that certain environmental events shaped their sexuality (such as the Oedipus complex in boys). Bieber *et al.* (1962) used Freudian concepts to explain the emergence of sexual orientation, by suggesting that homosexuals were likely to have mothers that were overly protective and doting, while their fathers were aggressive and unfeeling.

## EVALUATIVE COMMENT

**The psychoanalytic explanation of homosexuality rests first on the acceptance of Freudian concepts and principles upon which it is based, and several critics have questioned the theory, especially on**

Sexual preferences – biology or culture?

**methodological grounds. The study by Bieber *et al.* (1962) is also based on a sample of maladjusted adults undergoing psychiatric treatment, who in addition recalled events from their childhood retrospectively, thus generating concerns over the reliability of their accounts. The study by Bell *et al.* (1981) (see the Study above) presents mixed support for a traditional Freudian view; although identification with the opposite-sex parent was of no major significance, both males and females in the San Francisco survey reported difficult relationships with their fathers. Gleitman *et al.* (1999) argued the need for longitudinal data where both parents and children are followed up over several decades, although such a study could be questioned on ethical grounds since it is somewhat intrusive and invades privacy.**

Further support for the role of the environment was presented by Blumstein and Schwartz (1977), who focused upon the development of bisexuality. They proposed three factors:

1. experimentation within a friendship setting, particularly among female bisexuals

2. a liberal hedonistic environment in which various sexual activities and practices can be freely tried without fear of persecution or judgement

3. a general philosophy or outlook on life that is open and embraces eroticism, and of which attitudes to sex represent merely one element.

As this study indicates, an environment that is conducive and supportive to expressing one's sexuality is of utmost importance, and the culture in which one is raised can either facilitate or inhibit this process. In the twenty-first century, attitudes on various issues concerning sexuality in general, and sexual orientation in particular, are for the most part open and accepting. Homosexuality is no longer the stigmatised area it once was, although there is still more to be done to educate people and remove the prejudices harboured by some individuals and groups in society. As with many other aspects that may be discussed under the nature–nurture debate in psychology, whether a person is bisexual, homosexual or heterosexual cannot be attributed solely to the impact of biology or environment, but rather is best seen as an interaction of the two.

# 1.6 Problems in relationships

Most relationships will, at some time or other, undergo difficulties that can in many cases, with the effort of both people, be overcome. Other relationships experience problems to such an extent that breakdown is inevitable and the couple decide to end their partnership. This section will explore some of the factors that lead to relationships experiencing difficulties or ending, together with looking at the ways in which couples may respond to the situation if and when it arises.

## REFLECTIVE Activity

Read back over the previous sections of this chapter and make a note of the possible sources for a relationship breaking down. Having identified relevant factors you should then consider in what ways the issue could be resolved, allowing the relationship to continue. For example, one factor involved in interpersonal attraction was, you may recall, similarity (in attitudes or lifestyle), and so one source of strain on a relationship may be a gradual dissimilarity of views. For instance, one of the people may decide to join a fitness club that takes them out of the home on a regular basis. In this case, the couple may be able to resolve the situation by compromising on how often the person goes training, and working at strengthening their attachment in other aspects of their lives, by agreeing to spend exclusive time together on particular occasions.

After attempting the above activity you may have arrived at factors such as jealousy, boredom, poor communication, sexual problems, domestic violence and drug/alcohol abuse. Some of these sources of potential conflict in a relationship will now be examined.

## Factors affecting breakdown

A common cause of conflict within many relationships is poor communication, which can arise when one of the partners feels unable to tell the other person about their wishes or worries, or may simply be poorly skilled at doing so. This can then be frustrating for the other person, who feels powerless to resolve the situation. In social exchange theory (Homans, 1961), discussed earlier in connection with relationship formation, this can lead to inequity since one partner may come to believe that the costs incurred (e.g. the couple no longer talk about issues together) outweigh the benefits. The major problem with poor communication is that it usually entails one member of the couple playing a 'passive' role, while all of the effort to regain the balance in the relationship is placed upon the 'active' partner. In time the couple may drift further apart, and the intimacy and closeness they once had dwindles.

Within intimate (long-term) relationships some issues appear to affect both males and females equally. For instance, both men and women tend to be upset by unfaithfulness as well as by the harmful consequences of domestic violence, which can involve physical or verbal abuse (Weber, 1992). Statistically, though, it is still the case that women are more likely to be victims of physical or sexual abuse within the home than are men (Muncie and McLaughlin, 2001). Some areas of conflict, though, appear to be more distressing for one of the people in the couple, and in this respect some gender differences have emerged. While much of this research has concentrated on heterosexual couples, the underlying factors may have relevance to homosexual relationships. Buss (1989), for instance, questioned a large sample of men and women, and found males to be more concerned with issues such as sexual rejection, while females were upset by an unloving partner. Other work on heterosexual partnerships has supported these findings, with men being upset by their partner rejecting their sexual advances, as well as expressing concern over the other person's moodiness or general unresponsiveness. Women on the other hand, disliked men forcing sex (thus demonstrating their insensitivity to moods), and were also upset when their feelings or views were discounted (Weber, 1992).

Sexual problems are another example of a situation of imbalance or inequity arising in a relationship, if one partner is unsympathetic to the feelings of the other. We have already discussed the issues pertaining to sexual attitudes and behaviour, and usually as an intimate relationship progresses, sexual activity is normally matched. However numerous difficulties can occur as a result of ill-health, stress or fatigue, which may often be beyond the control of the couple. These can include specific problems such as erectile dysfunction (the inability to sustain an erection during intercourse) or female sexual dysfunction (a sudden loss of interest in sex that may persist for weeks or months). With a positive approach, though, these problems can be overcome. In addition to marriage guidance counsellors and organisations such as Relate, sexual therapists can provide professional help with many aspects of sexual problems. These can be quite diverse and range from dealing with specific dysfunctions such as those mentioned, to communication problems within a sexual relationship, or strategies to alleviate guilt experienced about sex (Reber, 2001).

Jealousy is particularly threatening to the stability of a relationship. As a negative emotional state it varies considerably between individuals and also between cultures, being more commonly found in societies that place great importance on sexual exclusivity, and where romantic partners are likely to be regarded as possessions (Weber, 1992). One cross-cultural study found that hugging someone of the opposite sex evokes much more jealousy from partners in Hungarian couples than those in the United States (Buunk and Hupka, 1987). In addition, jealousy is closely related to an individual's self-esteem since a person with low self-worth is more likely to feel threatened by their partner displaying affection to someone of the opposite sex. Although both males and females experience jealousy within intimate relationships, it has been found to be triggered by different reasons. Buss *et al.* (1992), for example, found that males are especially upset by their partner's unfaithfulness, whereas for females the actual unfaithful act itself is less distressing than the potential threat of emotional closeness with someone else.

Gender differences are also evident in the response to such events. Males tend to vent their feelings outwards, becoming angry and aggressive, and deflecting the blame on to their partner rather than themselves, while attempting to restore the situation by making their partner jealous in return. In contrast, women are more likely to cope by directing their feelings inwards, becoming depressed, placing the blame for the situation upon themselves, and coping by taking positive steps to strengthen the stability of the relationship (Weber, 1992).

**Study 1.7**

**AIM** Hill, Rubin and Peplau (1975) investigated the main factors involved in a relationship being terminated.

**METHOD** They conducted a longitudinal study based on 231 dating couples, just less than half of whom had ended their relationship approximately two years later.

**RESULT** Several factors emerged that were linked to the break-up, including differences in age, intelligence and physical attractiveness, as well as an imbalance in how much each person valued the relationship. The authors noted significant differences also in the level of negative exchange between the couples, those who split up being less able to deal effectively with any conflict that arose. Furthermore, such couples were more likely to adopt a negative attributional style, directing the blame when things went wrong on to their partner while at the same time not crediting them when events had a positive outcome.

**CONCLUSION** Relationships seem to be more likely to end when partners adopt a negative perspective, focusing all of their attention upon what is going wrong rather than taking positive steps to rectify the situation.

## Strategies when relationships break down

When a relationship is on the verge of dissolution a number of strategies are still, in theory, possible, before the end is accepted as inevitable. Rusbult and Zembrodt (1983) proposed four responses to confronting a failing relationship based around passivity and activity. These are:

1. *loyalty*, where one or both members of the pair passively respond by hoping that circumstances will somehow improve

2. *neglect*, where one or both members of the pair respond to their situation by ignoring it and thus passively allowing circumstances to worsen

3. *voice*, where one or both members of the pair make an active effort to do something in order to improve the failing relationship, by voicing their concerns to each other, say

4. *exit*, where one member of the couple realises that the relationship is irreparable, and rather than prolonging the situation makes an active decision to leave.

## PRACTICAL Activity

Many topics that you will have discovered in your studies involve lists of stages or headings such as those in the theory above. Trying to remember all of this information can sometimes be difficult and so one strategy that may help is to devise a mnemonic (memory aid). This can be done by taking the first letter of each of the words in the sequence and then making up a more memorable phrase that will later assist you in recalling the first letters of the terms you need. You may already be familiar with 'old age pensioners love grapes' as an aid to recalling 'OAPLG', the first letters for each of Freud's psychosexual stages. Try to devise a suitable mnemonic for the four responses proposed by Rusbult and Zembrodt (1983), and then do the same for the slightly more difficult model that follows.

Hatfield *et al.* (1982) based their model of responses to breakdown in terms of economic approaches such as equity theory and social exchange. In it, four strategies are identified, and just as with the previous theory, the actual termination of the relationship is seen as the last possible resort once every other technique has been tried and has failed. The first response is to assess the outcomes from the relationship compared with the inputs. If these are considered to be too low then the person may make certain demands from their partner, or negotiate, in order to boost them. Second, a person may alter their inputs into the relationship and so by reducing their efforts and commitment the outcomes now appear more appropriate. Third, the imbalance may be resolved by altering the way that the relationship is viewed so that a more realistic perspective is adopted, resulting in outcomes seeming fair. Finally, if balance cannot be established through changing how the relationship is perceived or by manipulating the outcomes or inputs, then equity will only be achieved by leaving.

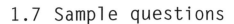

# 1.7 Sample questions

## SAMPLE QUESTION

(a) Some psychologists have suggested that human relationships develop in stages. Outline *one* criticism of this suggestion.

(AO1 = 1, AO2 = 2) *(3 marks)*

(b) Identify and describe *two* features of the triangular theory of love.

(AO1 = 4, AO2 = 0) *(4 marks)*

(c) Discuss the contention that a person's sexual orientation is determined by biological factors.

(AO1 = 5, AO2 = 8) *(13 marks)*

Total AO1 marks = 10  Total AO2 marks = 10  Total = 20 marks

## QUESTIONS, ANSWERS AND COMMENTS

(a) Explain the role of self-disclosure in the development of relationships.

(AO1 = 2, AO2 = 1) *(3 marks)*

(b) Describe *one* study in which the role of physical attractiveness in interpersonal attraction was investigated. In your answer you should refer to why the study was conducted, the method used, the results obtained and the conclusions drawn.

(AO1 = 4, AO2 = 1) *(5 marks)*

(c) Discuss *two* factors that may contribute to the breakdown of intimate relationships.

(AO1 = 4, AO2 = 8) *(12 marks)*

Total AO1 marks = 10  Total AO2 marks = 10  Total = 20 marks

# Answer to (a)

Self-disclosure is the term used in relationships when people reveal private personal things about themselves to the another person.

**Comment:** Two marks are awarded for this answer because it provides an acceptable definition of the term. Both marks are awarded for AO1 (knowledge and understanding). The third mark (for AO2) was lost because the candidate did not answer the question fully by giving an explanation of the role that self-disclosure plays in developing relationships, such as signalling that the relationship has progressed to a point where one person feels able to trust the other.

# Answer to (b)

Walster *et al.* carried out a field experiment to look at physical attractiveness. They arranged for students to go on a blind date and each person was matched up with a partner by a computer. When the students were later asked if they would be likely to see the person from their date again it was found that the most important factor affecting this was whether they thought the person was physically attractive or not.

**Comment:** This answer was awarded 3 marks (2 out of a possible 4 for AO1 and 1 mark for AO2). 1 mark was given for the method, which although not highly detailed does convey the procedure involved quite effectively. In addition the candidate was credited with a mark for AO2 for having identified the actual research method used. The third mark (AO1) was awarded for the reference to the results obtained in the study. The candidate did not provide a clear aim as to why the study was carried out, nor did they give a conclusion, so the remaining 2 marks for AO1 were not awarded.

# Answer to (c)

A number of factors have been shown to be involved in the breakdown of intimate relationships. These include boredom, jealousy and sexual problems. Jealousy can be very harmful to a relationship because the person who feels jealous of their partner may start to interpret everything in a negative way, and it is more likely in people who have low self-esteem. Jealousy does not affect everyone in the same way, though, as some people do not feel threatened by seeing their partner giving their attention to someone else, and it is more common in relationships where there is no trust. Studies have shown that it is also influenced by the culture that a person is raised in. For example, Buunk found that people from Hungary got more upset if their partner hugged someone of the opposite sex compared with people from America. However, it is difficult to generalise from this study because it only looked at two countries and so the findings may be different in other parts of the world. Also there are individual differences in how people feel about situations like this and not everyone in a culture is likely to behave in the same way.

Another problem in relationships is when difficulties occur that affect the couple's sex life. Sex is an important part of the relationship for an intimate couple, so if something happens that prevents one person from having sex then it will lead to problems. Some of the problems that can occur are when people experience stress at work so that this is on their mind all the time. Also people generally lead busy lives and often both people have a career, which means that they could be too tired.

Both of these problems can lead to a relationship breaking up but usually this is a last resort. Rusbult *et al.* said that it depends on how the couple respond to their difficulties as relationships are more likely to end if the couple are passive and just let things happen rather than trying to do something about it.

**Comment:** This answer was awarded 7 marks (out of 12). The candidate displays knowledge and understanding of two relevant issues, and in addition demonstrates some degree of application and analysis via their evaluation of the cross-cultural study cited. They have also attempted to appraise the area (albeit to a limited extent) in the last paragraph, which shows an effort to present a coherent argument. The answer tends to be unbalanced, though, and presents rather more psychological content in the coverage of jealousy. On occasion, the answer tends to be anecdotal and lacks a thorough use of psychological content and terminology. Improvements to be made would include further critical comments and evaluation; the inclusion of more in-depth coverage of relevant research would also be useful. Of the 7 marks, 4 marks were awarded for AO1 and 3 marks for AO2.

# 1.8 FURTHER READING

Introductory texts

Baron, R.A. & Byrne, D. 2002: **Social Psychology**. 10th Ed. Allyn & Bacon, Boston MA

Brehm, S.S. & Kassin, S.M. 1996: **Social Psychology**. 3rd Ed. Houghton Mifflin Company, Boston MA

Dwyer, D. 2000: **Interpersonal Relationships**. Routledge/Taylor & Francis, London

Pennington, D.C., Gillen, K. & Hill, P. 1999: **Social Psychology**. 2nd Ed. Arnold, London

## Specialist sources

Dindia, K. and Duck, S. (eds) 2000: **Communication in Personal Relationships**. Wiley & Sons Limited, Chichester

Duck, S. 1991: **Understanding Relationships**. Guildford Press, Guildford

Duck, S . 1999: **Relating to Others**. Oxford University Press, Oxford

Ickes, W. & Duck, S. (eds) 2000: **The Social Psychology of Personal Relationships**. Wiley & Sons Limited, Chichester

# 2

# Psychology and paranormal phenomena

## 2.1 What is parapsychology?

In modern society, everywhere we turn we are faced with 'science' in one form or another. The television and radio are full of programmes designed to keep us up to date with the latest scientific findings. However, there are some situations where scientific explanations seem to be inadequate. The term 'paranormal' is used to refer to situations where normal scientific explanations do not appear to provide a satisfactory answer. In this context, 'para-' means 'beyond', so in other words, paranormal refers to events or experiences that are 'beyond' the normal range of human experience. Scientists and psychologists have developed an understanding of human capabilities that is based on conventional science. Our five human senses of vision, smell, hearing, taste and touch are capable of performing certain functions but they also have their ilimitations. For example, our visual system is not capable of seeing ultraviolet light rays. However, some of the experiences people report seem to be difficult to explain if we rely on our conventional understanding of human capabilities. Many of us have heard of people who claim to have a 'sixth sense', which gives them abilities that extend beyond what is normally recognised as being possible. Parapsychology aims to investigate such phenomena in a systematic and rigorous fashion.

**Study 2.1**

**AIM** Blackmore (1997) set out to investigate the extent to which adults in the United Kingdom believed in the paranormal.

**METHOD** Participants were recruited using an appeal in a national newspaper; 6238 participants completed a questionnaire designed to find out whether or not they believed in the paranormal.

**RESULT** A total of 59 per cent of respondents were believers in the paranormal. There was a large sex difference, with 70 per cent of females believing in the paranormal, but only 48 per cent of males believing in the paranormal.

**CONCLUSION** The findings suggest that large numbers of the general public believe in the existence of paranormal phenomena.

The findings of Blackmore (1997) are similar to those of a survey carried out in the United States, which found that 49 per cent of American adults believe in the paranormal (Gallup and Newport, 1991). Both these studies seem to indicate that there is widespread belief in the paranormal. It is therefore important that psychologists and other scientists try to establish the validity of paranormal phenomena. There is a distinction between para-normal phenomena and paranormal experience. The term 'paranormal phenomena' refers to claims that there is a real effect occurring – for example, claims that telepathy really exists. On the other hand, the term 'paranormal experience' refers to the way in which individuals interpret their experiences as being paranormal. Even if paranormal phenomena do not exist, paranormal experiences clearly do – for example, in Gallup and Newport's (1991) survey, approximately 16 per cent of respondents claimed to have seen a UFO. In parapsychology, people who believe in the paranormal are referred to as 'sheep' while those who disbelieve are referred to as 'goats'.

In parapsychology, those who believe in the paranormal are referred to as 'sheep' and those who do not believe are referred to as 'goats'

There are two types of unusual event that form the basis of much research in parapsychology. The first type of event is when people acquire information in ways that cannot be explained by our current understanding of our sensory systems. This is often referred to as extra-sensory perception (ESP). The second type of event concerns affecting objects at a distance in ways not recognised by conventional science. This is usually referred to as psychokinesis (PK).

## Extra-sensory perception (ESP)

Telepathy, clairvoyance and precognition are the three basic types of ESP. Each of these is described below.

### TELEPATHY

Telepathy is basically the ability to read someone else's mind – or, stated another way, it is the extra-sensory perception of another person's thoughts.

## REFLECTIVE Activity

Have you or any of your friends ever had the experience of thinking about somebody and then receiving a text or telephone call from them, or seeing them? This is often considered to be one form of telepathy. If this has happened to you or your friends is there an alternative explanation, other than telepathy, that could be used to account for the experience?

One form of telepathy is referred to as 'call' experiences. These are experiences in which an individual hears someone whom they love calling their name even though that person is some distance away. Typically the person doing the 'calling' is in some form of distress. One of the questions posed by cases like this is who is responsible for the telepathic experience. Is the person 'calling' responsible in some way for sending a message, or is the person receiving the message in some way seeking out information on people who are emotionally close to them? Rhine (1956) argues that in 'call' experiences information is being actively sought by the person who is called rather than being sent by the person in distress.

| Type of extra-sensory perception (ESP) | Description |
| --- | --- |
| Telepathy | Information is sent from one person to another without using any of the recognised five senses |
| Clairvoyance | A person gains information about an object that is hidden from view without using any of the recognised five senses |
| Precognition | A person knows about an event before it occurs; the knowledge could not have been gained from existing information |

Figure 2.2: Types of extra-sensory perception

## CLAIRVOYANCE

In some situations the extra-sensory experience is not concerned with information in someone else's mind but with something that is either hidden from view or some distance away. Clairvoyance is the ability to perceive events or objects that are not accessible using our normal senses. One of the most famous clairvoyants was a Polish engineer called Stefan Ossowiecki. He was tested extensively in the 1920s and 1930s in the following manner. A target drawing with a title was produced, folded over and placed in a sealed package. The package was then given to Ossowiecki by someone who knew nothing about the contents or about the nature of the study. This meant that Ossowiecki could not pick up any clues from the person who gave him the package. Ossowiecki was very successful at identifying what the drawing was without opening the package. Unfortunately, Ossowiecki was killed in 1944, during the Second World War.

## PRECOGNITION

Precognition refers to the extra-sensory awareness of a future event or, more simply, it is the ability to accurately predict future events. Precognitive experiences tend to be concerned with events that have some emotional significance for the person who experiences them. Writings about precognition have a long history – for example, Pharaoh's dream about seven fat cows and seven lean cows, recorded in the Bible, seems to have the characteristics of a precognitive vision. The majority of precognitive experiences seem to take the form of dreams. For example, Rhine (1954) found that 75 per cent of reported precognitive experiences took the form of realistic dreams. Other forms of precognitive experience reported include hallucinations and intuitions or feelings that something was about to happen. The time between the precognitive experience and the event actually occurring is typically a matter of days. For example, Orme (1974) reported that about half of the events identified in precognitive experiences occurred within two days.

**Study 2.2**

**AIM** Stowell (1997) set out to investigate the characteristics of precognitive dreams.

**METHOD** Five women who had reported experiencing precognitive dreams were interviewed. One of the participants was aged 19 years and the others were in their forties and fifties.

**RESULT** Four types of dream were identified. One type provided information about non-traumatic situations, whereas the second type appeared to provide some form of guidance for the dreamer. The third type related to negative situations where it was not possible for the dreamer to intervene or take any action. The final type provided information about situations where it was possible for the dreamer to intervene in some way.

**CONCLUSION** The findings provide a system for categorising precognitive dreams, which can be used in future research. The findings also provide the basis for developing a better understanding of the nature of the precognitive dreams experienced by some people.

Because precognitive experiences are related to the future it is possible to investigate whether or not they are accurate. Since being able to predict the future clearly has a number of benefits, a number of groups referred to as 'premonition bureaux' have been set up. The idea is that people with premonitions are invited to give the information to one of the bureaux before the event takes place. However, the percentage of registered premonitions that turn out to be correct is very low (Irwin, 1999).

## EVALUATIVE COMMENT

**Deciding how to classify ESP experiences can often be quite difficult. Consider the following experience. I am thinking about a friend I have not heard from for quite a few months. Later the same day I receive a postcard from him. If this experience was interpreted as an extra-sensory awareness of the postcard itself then it could be classified as a clairvoyant experience. It could be interpreted as a telepathic experience on the grounds that I was aware of the thoughts of my friend. On the other hand it could be classified as a precognitive experience, predicting the arrival of a postcard. As a result of problems classifying ESP the term 'general extra-sensory perception' (GESP) was used to refer to experiences that could have components of one or more of the three forms of ESP.**

## Psychokinesis (PK)

Psychokinesis (PK) literally translated means 'movement by the mind'. Unlike ESP phenomena, which are primarily concerned with receiving information, PK is concerned with the way in which the mind of an individual can influence physical objects. It can be expressed more simply using the phrase 'mind over matter'. The incidence of spontaneously occurring PK phenomena appears to be relatively low. Rhine (1963a) collected over 10 000 reports of paranormal experiences and only 178 of these were of PK experiences. More recently, Palmer (1979) conducted a survey of paranormal experiences; approximately 50 per cent of these were ESP experiences whereas only 7 per cent were PK experiences.

A commonly reported PK experience appears to be a watch or clock stopping when a relative or friend dies. Other occurrences include objects breaking – for example, in one case reported by Rhine (1961), a light bulb exploded for no apparent reason. The woman who experienced this found out a few days later that at the time the light bulb exploded her brother's house had been destroyed by fire. The assumption made in events such as these is that the physical events are the result of the PK abilities of an individual.

# PRACTICAL Activity

Ask your friends and family if any of them have experienced PK phenomena such as a clock stopping when someone has died. If anyone has had such an experience, is there an alternative explanation for the events that occurred?

| Type of physical event reported | Frequency |
|---|---|
| Objects falling (e.g. off a shelf) | 36% |
| Clocks stopping or starting | 27% |
| Objects breaking or exploding | 12% |
| Lights turning off or on | 10% |
| Doors opening, shutting or unlocking | 8% |
| Objects rocking or shaking | 7% |

**Figure 2.3:** The types and frequency of PK activities reported by Rhine (1963a)

Nearly all the 178 PK experiences reported by Rhine (1963a) involved two people: one who observed the physical effect and one who was some distance away undergoing some sort of

Psychokinesis is the ability to influence physical objects using only your mind. In the 1970s Uri Geller appeared on television and appeared to demonstrate an ability to bend spoons and keys; many experts now believe his abilities were due to trickery rather than psychokinesis

crisis. Typically the two people involved were close friends or relatives. The most common event reported involved objects falling – for example, mirrors and paintings falling off the wall and objects falling off shelves. The full set of categories and their relative frequencies are shown in Figure 2.3.

In recent years a considerable amount of interest in PK has been generated by the exploits of Uri Geller. Geller appeared on several television programmes during the 1970s, and appeared to bend spoons and keys using PK. In general, Geller has been rather reluctant to take part in carefully controlled experiments (Irwin, 1999) and there are documented instances of him cheating (Hutchinson, 1988). Nevertheless, as Beloff (1993) points out, 'Geller succeeded in putting the paranormal squarely on the map for perhaps the first time in living memory' (1993: 199). However, interest in Geller's spoon-bending exploits has gradually declined, leaving only a number of unanswered questions.

## EVALUATIVE COMMENT

**If PK is an authentic phenomena then it is interesting to speculate what effect it might have on the process of doing reliable and valid experiments in parapsychology. Suppose the person conducting the research has PK abilities. This gives rise to the possibility that they could**

consciously or unconsciously influence the equipment being used in the experiment. This in turn could result in the generation of data that supports the hypothesis being tested. Even more extreme is the possibility that the experimenter could exert some control over the responses of the participant. Many of the phenomena in parapsychology overlap to a certain extent, which gives rise to the use of different terms to describe them. For example, 'psi phenomena' is a term that includes both PK and ESP.

## 2.2 Research methods in parapsychology

### Case studies

The case-study approach to research typically involves the in-depth study of particular instances or cases. In order to develop a good understanding of the case, psychologists will usually collect a considerable amount of descriptive material. It is possible to identify two ways in which case studies have been used in parapsychological research. First, they have been used in the standard way – that is, the in-depth investigation of individual cases. This could involve the study of a person who appears to have particular abilities, but on the other hand it could also involve the investigation of a particular occurrence. The Society for Psychical Research (SPR) was founded in England in 1882 by a group of people who believed that claims for the existence of paranormal activity should be investigated scientifically (Irwin, 1999).

One of the early activities of the SPR was to develop a set of criteria that could be used in the collection of reports on spontaneous parapsychological experiences. Spontaneous experiences are those that occur unexpectedly in people's everyday lives rather than in artificial settings such as experimental laboratories. This means that it is very difficult to ensure that accurate information is collected. The most basic criteria specified by the SPR was that there should be some record of the experience, preferably in writing but at the very least someone must have been told about the experience. If the case was considered to be worthy of further investigation, then a team of SPR members would carry out an investigation. This would take the form of interviews with any witnesses or other people who were involved, and the collection of any relevant documents. The main aim of the investigation was to try and make sure that the information was accurate and the evidence reliable.

The second way in which case studies have been used in parapsychology has been to collect a large number of cases that have something in common – for example, cases where people have experienced PK or ESP. This approach enables researchers to look for similarities and commonalities among the cases.

**Study 2.3**

**AIM** Rhine (1953) set out to investigate the characteristics of spontaneous ESP experiences.

**METHOD** Approximately 1000 cases of spontaneous ESP experiences were collected and analysed.

**RESULT** Four main types of spontaneous ESP experience were found: (1) intuitive (a simple unreasoned impression or hunch); (2) hallucinations; (3) unrealistic dreaming (characterised by fantasy); (4) realistic dreaming (characterised by photographically realistic imagery).

**CONCLUSION** The findings were used to support the view that spontaneous ESP experiences resemble normal cognitive processes.

Rhine's (1953) study is an example of combining a large number of cases in an attempt to identify particular characteristics of paranormal experiences. One of the major outcomes of the study was that it provided a better understanding of the nature and frequency of spontaneous ESP phenomena. The study also provided some insight into what it is like for people to have an ESP experience.

## EVALUATIVE COMMENT

**The early case studies were mainly concerned with establishing the authenticity of the experiences. However, interest began to develop into the nature and characteristics of parapsychological experiences. Irwin (1999) points out the advantages and disadvantages of using spontaneous case studies in parapsychological research. The advantages are, first, that they reflect 'real life' experiences rather than an artificial environment created in a laboratory. Second, they are useful in identifying the different ways in which ESP and PK can be expressed. Third, they can provide the basis for generating hypotheses that can be tested experimentally. Finally they provide us with some insight into the subjective experience of paranormal phenomena.**

**The limitations of spontaneous case material are, first, people's recall of events can often be inaccurate. Second, the way in which people perceive events is subject to a number of biases. For example, our perception is influenced by our expectations, and beliefs are not very good at making judgements about probability. For example, many of us have a belief that old houses could be haunted. So if we spend a night in an unfamiliar old house then we are more likely to perceive naturally occurring noises as paranormal activity. Third, case reports can often be subject to deception and fraud. There are certainly some reported cases that have been intentionally constructed in an attempt to deceive people. This can be done for several reasons: sometimes professional psychics deceive an audience for financial gain, on other occasions people are simply trying to deceive the researchers.**

## Experimental (laboratory) procedures

A central concern in parapsychological research is authenticity. In other words, are the paranormal experiences reported by people due to factors as yet unknown to conventional science? One way of shedding some light on this situation is to use experimental methods. Experiments form the basis for conventional scientific research and mainstream psychological research. So the use of carefully controlled experiments might be one way of ensuring that the claims made by parapsychologists are taken seriously by other scientists and the general public. Although early research into paranormal phenomena relied heavily on field investigations and case studies, it soon became clear that issues of authenticity could only be addressed by the use of experimental procedures.

One of the most influential figures in the development of experimental procedures in parapsychology was Joseph Banks Rhine. He was responsible for setting up one of the first experimental laboratories designed exclusively for parapsychological research. A major aim of Rhine's research programme was to demonstrate that psychic ability was not restricted to a few gifted individuals but was much more widespread. One of the issues that has to be addressed by researchers designing parapsychological experiments is 'sensory leakage'. Sensory leakage refers to the possibility that participants can pick up information through their normal senses. For example, in a study involving playing cards, if the backs of the playing cards are visible to the participant there is the possibility that there might be some marks that enable the participant to identify a card or cards. There are many other ways in which sensory leakage could occur, such as participants overhearing conversations between the experimenters, which could give them some indication of the target material.

## REFLECTIVE Activity

Consider the implications for conducting experiments in parapsychology if ESP and PK really exist.

What would be the effect on the results if the participant could read the experimenter's mind?

What would be the consequences if the experimenter could use PK to influence the instruments being used in the research?

In the majority of experiments in parapsychology, participants' performance on a task is compared with the results that you would expect to get by chance. A simple example of this would be a coin-tossing task. If we toss a coin in the air we would expect it to land on 'heads' 50 per cent of the time and 'tails' for the other 50 per cent. If there is something influencing the way the coin lands other than chance then the pattern would be different. For example, if someone claimed to have PK powers then perhaps we could test their claims by asking them to influence a coin tossed in the air so that it landed on 'heads'. If we did this and found that 60 per cent of the time the coin landed on heads we might believe their claim. In other words we would be saying that the participant's PK abilities caused the coin to land on 'heads' more than you

Sensory leakage is potentially a problem in parapsychological experiments; any possibility that the participant could pick up information using their normal senses must be avoided; in experiments using cards there is always the possibility that some mark or pattern on the back of the card might provide a clue to its identity

would expect by chance. But are there any other possible explanations that could be used to account for the results? Indeed there are! A few possibilities are: there could be something to do with the coin that meant that it landed on 'heads' more often than 'tails'; the person tossing the coin in the air could be intentionally or unintentionally influencing the way the coin landed; the experimenter could have misrecorded the results, intentionally or unintentionally. So before we can identify a causal relationship between the participant's PK abilities and the results we must rule out all the alternative explanations.

## EVALUATIVE COMMENT

**One of the problems with research findings in parapsychology is that many of them cannot be replicated (Hyman, 1989). However, it must also be pointed out that replicability is also a problem for mainstream psychology, since many influential experiments have also proved difficult to replicate. In parapsychological experiments conducted on the general population it is expected that the size of any effects will be rather small. One of the ways in which small effects can be detected is to ensure that the participants complete a large number of trials. A technique called 'meta-analysis' has also been used in situations where the size of the effects is relatively small and the results of experiments somewhat unreliable. Essentially the technique involves combining the results from all the available experiments that have looked at the same phenomena. Because meta-analysis enables small effects to be more reliably identified it is appropriate to use in parapsychology.**

## Field investigations

A third approach to investigating paranormal phenomena consists of the use of field investigations. In field investigations, researchers collect data in naturalistic settings. In some situations this is a positive choice on the part of the researchers; a field investigation is considered to be the best way of investigating the phenomena of interest. In other situations the researchers are left with no other choice – for example, the participant might not be willing or able to take part in a laboratory study. Irwin (1999) describes the case of a Russian psychic called Nina Kulagina who was brought to the attention of parapsychologists during the late 1960s. Nina was apparently capable of moving objects using PK. A team of parapsychologists visited her in Moscow, but at this time the Russian authorities did not want to be seen to be encouraging research into the paranormal. Consequently, the investigations of Nina's abilities were conducted in her own apartment. Although the researchers (Keil *et al.*, 1976) confirmed that her ability to move objects without touching them appeared to be genuine, their research lacked the control that would have been possible in a laboratory.

Some paranormal phenomena are extremely difficult to study in the laboratory – for example, ghosts and apparitions. Stories of ghosts and other apparitions are common in many cultures. Such phenomena have formed the basis for a significant amount of field research into the paranormal. Typically this involves setting up some specialist equipment in places where an apparition has been reported to appear. One of the aims is to try and identify some objective evidence, such as rapid changes in temperature, that could be used to support the existence of paranormal activity. Recent research into apparitions was carried out at Edinburgh Castle.

## Study 2.4

**AIM** Wiseman *et al.* (in press) set out to investigate why some people report 'ghostly' experiences such as the sense of a presence, apparitions and feelings of intense cold, in places with a reputation for being haunted.

**METHOD** Participants were asked to stand in the underground vaults of Edinburgh Castle and to report any unusual phenomena they experienced. Some of the vaults have a reputation for being haunted, others do not. Participants were not aware of the reputation of the vaults. Physical characteristics of the vaults, such as size and lighting, were also measured.

**RESULT** A total of 51 per cent of the participants in vaults with a reputation for being haunted reported unusual experiences, against only 35 per cent of participants in vaults without a reputation for being haunted. The vaults with a reputation for being haunted were larger in terms of floor space and height, and also had darker corridors leading to them, than those vaults without this reputation.

**CONCLUSION** The results were taken to support the view that the vaults with a reputation for being haunted were experienced differently from those without this reputation. The physical characteristics (size and lighting) were assumed to be responsible for the differences.

Recently there has been an increase in the use of media such as newspapers and the Internet as a means of collecting large amounts of data. These approaches could be considered to be a form of field investigation in the sense that they collect data from people in their normal environment. These studies are often referred to as 'mass media' studies and typically involve people sitting at home trying to guess the identity of a distant target. A recent meta-analysis of mass-media tests of ESP was carried out by Milton and Wiseman (1999a). Their findings provided no evidence of ESP under the conditions used in mass-media studies. These findings are in contrast to other meta-analyses, which have provided support for the existence of ESP. There are two possible interpretations of Milton and Wiseman's (1999a) findings. One explanation could be that mass-media studies do not provide appropriate conditions for the demonstration of ESP. An alternative explanation is that ESP does not exist. Regardless of which interpretation is correct, the findings provide no evidence of psychic functioning under the conditions used in mass-media studies.

## EVALUATIVE COMMENT

**Field research has the advantage that researchers can study behaviour in the locations where it actually occurs rather than creating an artificial environment in a laboratory. It is also the case that some paranormal phenomena, such as apparitions, would be extremely difficult to study in a laboratory. In recent years some attempts have been made to induce apparitional experiences in the laboratory. The procedure involves the participant thinking about a dead person they would like to see again. The participant then relaxes and looks into a mirror that is positioned so they can see the wall behind them. The participants in a study conducted by Radin and Rebman (1996) reported sensing the presence of the dead person rather than a vivid apparitional experience.**

## Experimenter effects and demand characteristics

The traditional approach to conducting experiments sees the researcher as being impartial, objective and separate from the participant. However, if ESP and PK really do exist, then the experimental setting becomes even more difficult to control than in normal psychology experiments. For example, it would be impossible to use 'blind' methods because they could be penetrated by someone with ESP. One of the interesting observations about experimental parapsychology is that some experimenters appear to consistently achieve positive results, while others do not appear to have any success. A cynical view would be that those researchers achieving positive results are either fraudulent or not very careful in the way they carry out their experiments. However, there is little evidence to support this cynical view (Watt, 2001). There is also some evidence that experimenters whose participants appear to do well on ESP and PK tasks also appear to do well themselves on such tasks.

Although experimenter effects are potentially a problem throughout the whole of experimental psychology, they are rather more complex in experimental parapsychology. There are two basic forms of experimenter effect: intentional and unintentional. One of the most drastic forms of an intentional experimenter effect is cheating, or faking the results. Fortunately, in both mainstream psychology and parapsychology this is a very rare occurrence. However, there is a variety of ways in which an experimenter can unintentionally have an impact on the results of an experiment. One of these is referred to as 'experimenter expectancy' and relates to the fact that the person running the experiment may be committed to producing a particular outcome.

Experimenter expectancy is clearly an issue in parapsychological research where experimenters tend to be either believers or disbelievers. Believers are clearly committed to proving that PK and ESP are real phenomena, whereas disbelievers are committed to disproving their existence. Blackmore (1985) points out that an experimenter effect in parapsychology experiments could be either the result of 'normal' processes present in any laboratory experiment or due to psychic phenomena. It could be the case that the beliefs of the experimenter are conveyed to the participants in normal ways such as through non-verbal cues. If the experimenters are disbelievers, then the participants could be inhibited when it comes to producing any paranormal phenomena. There is also some evidence to suggest that ESP is more likely to be demonstrated in laboratories where there is a friendly atmosphere (Crandall, 1985). So experimenter effects refer to the potential impact that the experimenter can have on the results of a particular experiment.

However, if ESP and PK do in fact exist, then the situation becomes much more complex. There are several ways in which this could result in an experimenter effect. For example, a non-believing experimenter could actually impress his beliefs on the participants by ESP and they would conform by producing no ESP or PK. On the other hand, the experimenter could affect the results directly by means of PK or ESP.

'Demand characteristics' were first identified by Orne (1962), who recognised that

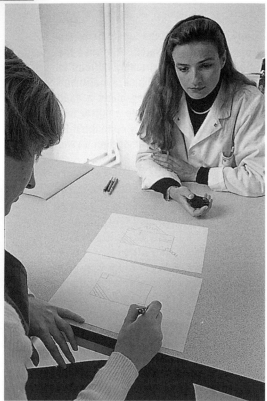

Experimenters can influence the results of parapsychological experiments in a variety of ways; occasionally this can be intentional but more often any 'experimenter effect' is unintentional; if ESP and PK do exist, then this makes coping with experimenter effects much more complex

experiments are in fact social situations. In social settings when people are confronted by an unusual or unfamiliar situation they try to make sense of it and decide what is going on. The same processes occur when people take part in an experiment, they react by trying to make sense of what is going on. Participants invariably try and work out what the experimenter is trying to do and in many cases try to be 'helpful' by providing the 'right' answers. Other participants may do the opposite and try to mess up the experiment by providing inappropriate information. So the term 'demand characteristics' refers to cues in the experimental setting that enable participants to guess the nature of the experiment or what is expected of them by the experimenter. So, in the case of parapsychology, participants are likely to work out the aims of the experiment quite easily, which in turn could affect their behaviour. The fact that believers tend to perform better than disbelievers could be used to support the view that demand characteristics affect the findings of parapsychology experiments.

## EVALUATIVE COMMENT

**Dealing with potential experimenter effects and demand characteristics is an ongoing problem for parapsychological research. It is difficult to see, given the nature of ESP and PK, how they can be satisfactorily resolved in an experimental setting. It is also interesting to note that some experimenters appear to be able to consistently produce significant results, whereas others consistently produce non-significant results. It would appear to be the case that the only way to control for potential experimenter effects in parapsychological research is for experimenters to conduct replications of each other's experiments. If a particular result is confirmed by several researchers then it becomes increasingly unlikely that the results are due to an experimenter effect (Irwin, 1999).**

## 2.3 Extra-sensory perception

A typical ESP experiment involves four components: target material, an 'agent' (sometimes referred to as a 'sender'), the experimenter, and the participant (see Figure 2.7). In modern ESP experiments, the agent and target material will usually be in a different room from the participant. The agent will focus on the target material, and the participant will try to identify the nature of the target material using ESP.

### Experimental methods and paradigms used in ESP research

The basic design underpinning all ESP experiments involves the selection of some target material by the experimenter that has to be identified by the participant using some form of ESP.

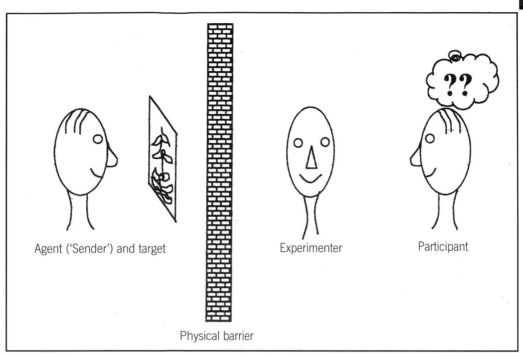

Figure 2.7: The main components of a typical ESP experiment

It is important that the participant should have no sensory access to the target material in order that sensory leakage can be avoided. Experimental investigations into ESP have used either a 'free-response' technique or a 'forced-choice' technique. In a free-response technique the participant is simply asked to verbally or visually describe the target material. In the forced-choice technique participants are aware of the set of targets they have to choose from – for example, a set of playing cards. One of the advantages of the forced-choice technique is that it means that a participant's performance can easily be converted to numbers, or quantified. An early study carried out using a forced-choice technique was reported by Gurney *et al.* (1886). In one of the studies they reported an agent concentrated on a playing card selected at random and the participant attempted to identify the card using telepathy. This type of study provides quantitative data – that is, the number of correct responses. It is also possible to calculate the probability of getting the answer correct. In theory, if the target material is a set of playing cards the probability of naming the card correctly by chance is 1 in 52. This means that the number of correct responses achieved by each participant can be compared with the number of correct responses you would expect to get by chance. If the two are significantly different then it can be used as evidence in support of the existence of ESP.

## PRACTICAL Activity

You will need a pack of playing cards and some willing friends or family members for this activity. Explain to each person that you would like to check out whether or not they have any powers of ESP. Pick a card at random from the deck of playing cards and look at it. Ask your friend to guess what the card is. Repeat this 104 times for each person!
Record the results on a sheet with the following headings:

| Actual card | Guess | Correct (yes/no) |
| --- | --- | --- |
|  |  |  |

Do particular cards appear to be guessed more often than others?

Do people appear to have a preference for some cards over others?

You would expect people to correctly guess two cards out of the 104 trials by chance. Have any people guessed more than two cards? If they have, do you think it constituted evidence for the existence of ESP?

One of the problems of using playing cards is that people appear to have a preference for some cards rather than others – for example, aces (Irwin, 1999). Another problem with playing cards is that they contain two pieces of information: the face value (ace, two, three, etc.) and the suit (diamonds, hearts, spades and clubs). So if a correct answer is only awarded to people who get both pieces of information correct then people do not get any credit for getting the suit or face value correct. In order to get around these problems Karl Zener designed a set of five cards, each with a different symbol on it: a cross, a square, a circle, a star, and wavy lines (see Figure 2.8) Not surprisingly the cards are referred to as Zener cards and a typical pack contains 25 cards, five of each symbol.

Various techniques have been developed to test different aspects of ESP using Zener cards. The 'down through' (DT) method is designed to measure clairvoyance; the participant has to guess the order of the symbols in a pack that has been shuffled and placed face down on a table. After the participant has made 25 guesses the cards are turned over and their score is calculated. Another procedure was designed to test clairvoyance and/or telepathy. In this technique the experimenter places the shuffled pack on a table, takes the top card, looks at it, and the participant has to guess the card.

In a free-response technique, participants are given a target that is a picture, an object or a real-life scene. But they are not provided with any additional information, in other words they are not choosing their answer from a restricted list of items as in the forced-choice technique. This means that what constitutes a 'hit', or correct answer, is rather more difficult to determine.

It depends on the extent to which an independent observer thinks that the participant's description matches the target. Clearly this is a very time-consuming and to a certain extent subjective process. However, one advantage of the free-response technique is that it is closer to the spontaneous occurrence of ESP reported by people than the forced-choice technique. Three types of free-response technique have been used extensively to study ESP: dream studies, the ganzfeld technique, and remote viewing.

Dream studies are often referred to as 'the Maimonides studies' because they were carried out at a laboratory set up at the Maimonides Hospital in the United States. The basic

Figure 2.8: Zener cards

procedure for conducting this type of research is as follows (see also Figure 2.9). The participant is connected to an electroencephalograph (EEG), which monitors brainwaves, and then goes to

| One trial consists of the following procedure. |
| --- |
| • Participant connected to EEG |
| • Participant goes to sleep in a soundproof room |
| • Participant starts to dream |
| • Agent looks at a picture selected at random in another room |
| • When participant stops dreaming, they are woken up and asked to describe their dream |
| • Procedure repeated every time the participant enters dream sleep |
| • In the morning, participant shown a set of pictures and asked to identify target picture |
| • Transcripts of tapes sent to independent judge to assess similarity with target picture |

Figure 2.9: Summary of the procedure used in the Maimonides dream studies

sleep in a soundproof room. In a different soundproof room, another person acts as the 'agent'. When the participant starts dreaming, the agent is given a picture to look at and think about. The next stage occurs when the participant emerges from the dream phase of their sleep; they are woken up and record their dreams using a tape-recorder. The participant is then allowed to go to sleep again and the procedure is repeated using the same picture. When the participant awakes the next morning, they are shown a set of pictures, including the target picture, and asked to identify the target picture. A full experiment could last a month or more, with each

night counting as a single trial. At the end of each experiment all the transcripts of the tape-recordings are sent to independent judges, who rate their similarity to the target pictures.

One of the questions that arose from the Maimonides studies concerned the role of external stimulation in ESP. One of the possible explanations for the successes was based on the fact that when people are sleeping the amount of stimulation from the environment is limited. It was suggested that stimulation from the environment might inhibit ESP, therefore reducing the amount of stimulation could make it easier for participants to demonstrate ESP effects. This view was supported by studies which indicate that techniques that relax the participant increase the chances of demonstrating a significant ESP effect (Braud, 1975). The fact that sensory deprivation produces a similar state to sleep was used by Honorton and Harper (1974) in a technique that is referred to as the 'ganzfeld technique'.

The ganzfeld technique has been used extensively in ESP research; the technique reduces the information received by our normal sensory systems; this appears to increase the likelihood of ESP occurring

The ganzfeld technique (see Figure 2.11) usually consists of participants wearing a set of translucent goggles (table tennis balls cut in half are often used) and a pair of headphones through which 'white noise' is played. White noise consists of sound containing all frequencies – for example, the hissing sound made by an FM radio tuned between stations. In a typical ganzfeld experiment, a target picture will be selected at random from a set of four pictures and viewed by an agent in a room separate from the participant. The participant will be left in a state of sensory deprivation for approximately 30 minutes. Then the goggles and headphones are removed and the participant will be asked to describe any images they had during the period of sensory deprivation. The descriptions can then be compared to the actual target. An alternative technique is to present the participants with all the stimulus pictures and ask them to decide which was the one being looked at by the agent. This enables the results to be quantified.

| One trial consists of the following procedure. |
|---|
| • Participant wears translucent goggles and headphones |
| • Agent in another room looks at a target picture selected at random |
| • After approximately 30 minutes the participant is asked to describe the target picture |
| • In some studies the participant is asked to select the target picture from a sample of other pictures |
| • Descriptions are compared to the target picture by independent observers |

Figure 2.11: Summary of the ganzfeld procedure

In response to criticisms concerning possible methodological problems in the ganzfeld technique, Charles Honorton developed a modified version of it called the 'autoganzfeld technique'. In the original ganzfeld method there is the possibility of sensory leakage when the participants are asked to select the target picture from a sample of other pictures. It is possible that the experimenter could unknowingly give the participant some cues as to which of the pictures is the target picture. In order to ensure that there is no sensory leakage taking place in the autoganzfeld technique, computers are used to control the presentation of material when the participant is being asked to identify the target. This means that there is no experimenter present when the participant makes their choice.

Remote viewing is another type of research that has used the free-response technique. In remote viewing the target is normally a real-life scene or object. This makes it closer to the real-life experiences of ESP. Remote viewing is basically a special form of clairvoyance, and consists of a person giving a description of buildings and landscapes rather than hidden objects such as cards or pictures. The standard remote-viewing task involves two researchers, one of whom remains with the participant (remote viewer) while the other drives to a randomly selected target site. It is important that the researcher that remains with the participant is not aware of the destination. If they do know the location then there is the possibility of them unknowingly giving clues to the participant. The participant is instructed to tell the researcher whatever is going through their mind, and sometimes the participant will use drawings to describe what they are experiencing. After several trials the descriptions are rated by independent judges to determine how well they describe the location.

# REFLECTIVE Activity

Think about the practical applications of remote viewing. If remote viewing is really possible how do you think the armed forces and could make use of someone who was capable of doing it? You might be interested to note that many countries around the world (for example, the USA, Russia and the UK) have funded research into remote viewing.

# EVALUATIVE COMMENT

**One of the disadvantages of using the free-response technique is that the data is typically qualitative, in the form of descriptions that have to be compared with the target picture. In such situations it is very difficult to determine the extent to which any similarity between the descriptions and the target are due to coincidence or ESP. For example, if someone describes a landscape then it is quite likely to have at least some features, such as trees and fences, that are common to many other landscapes. Several problems have been identified with research that has used Zener cards. There is the possibility that if the participants can see the backs of the cards they might pick up sensory cues – for example, there might be slight differences in the patterns on the cards, which could be used to identify the card or cards. If you shuffle a deck of cards some of them often do not get separated and stay in the same order. This is clearly a problem if you are repeatedly using the same deck of cards. More recently this problem has been overcome by the use of computers to randomly generate the target symbols. It is interesting to note that significant results are still obtained in this way. Another problem concerns the use of the 5 per cent significance level. When you use this level you are accepting the fact that if you run 20 experiments you would expect by chance to get one significant result. So critics have argued that the significant results merely reflect chance fluctuations in the scores. One way of contesting this claim is for parapsychological research laboratories to make all their experimental data available for inspection by others.**

## Personality traits and ESP

Two aspects of personality that have been investigated in relation to ESP are neuroticism and extraversion. Neurotic people tend to be anxious and tense, or rely heavily on ways of protecting themselves against the effects of anxiety (usually referred to as 'defence mechanisms'). In general there seems to be a negative correlation between ESP performance and high levels of neuroticism, whereas people who are well adjusted and stable tend to demonstrate ESP scores above chance (Irwin, 1999). One measure of neuroticism that has been used extensively in ESP research is a projective test called the 'defence mechanism test' (DMT). People who score highly on the DMT usually have a tendency to suffer from anxiety.

**Study 2.5**

**AIM** Johnson and Haraldsson (1984) designed an experiment to investigate the relationship between ESP performance and levels of neuroticism as measured by the DMT.

**METHOD** A total of 54 male undergraduates were given the DMT and an ESP test that consisted of a precognition test and a clairvoyance test, both of which used computer-generated targets with immediate and continuous feedback.

**RESULT** There was a significant negative correlation between the DMT and the ESP scores. People with high DMT scores were less successful on the ESP tests than people with low DMT scores.

**CONCLUSION** The results were taken to support the view that ESP could be associated with some kind of subconscious processing responsible for people's level of anxiety and neuroticism.

Following the successful demonstration of a significant negative correlation between neuroticism and ESP Johnson and Haraldsson (1984) conducted another study using a different set of participants. The results of this study were not significant. However, a subsequent meta-analysis of these and other studies investigating the relationship between DMT scores and ESP performance provided evidence for a significant negative correlation (Haraldsson and Houtkooper, 1992). Watt (2001) argues that this provides evidence that ESP information could

Extraverts are more likely to do well on ESP tests than introverts; it is not clear why this appears to be the case, but perhaps it might be something to do with how relaxed people feel in the experimental setting; extraverts might feel at ease more readily than introverts, and are therefore more likely to use their ESP abilities

be processed according to normal psychological principles. If this view is correct then it is important because it offers the possibility of integrating parapsychological research and findings with existing psychological theory.

Extraversion has been found to be positively correlated with ESP performance. In other words, people who are extraverts are more likely to do well on ESP tests than people who are introverts. Honorton, Ferrari and Bem (1998) carried out a meta-analysis on 60 studies that had looked at the relationship between extraversion and performance on ESP tasks. They found that in experiments using a free-response method there was a significant correlation between extraversion and performance on ESP tasks. However, in experiments using a forced-choice method the correlation was not significant. Thus, the way in which ESP is tested appears to have an influence on whether or not a significant correlation is found between extraversion and ESP performance.

The relationship between personality and ESP performance is further complicated by the fact that there appears to be a difference between the personality of believers (sheep) and disbelievers (goats). Thalbourne and Haraldsson (1980) found that 'sheep' tended to be more extravert than 'goats'. There is also some evidence that 'sheep' tend to be more neurotic than 'goats' (Thalbourne, 1981). Lawrence (1993) conducted a meta-analysis of 73 studies, which looked at differences in outcome between 'sheep' and 'goats'. His findings showed that believers performed consistently better than non-believers in parapsychological experiments.

## EVALUATIVE COMMENT

**The relationship between neuroticism and ESP scores appears to hold true only for settings where the ESP testing is done on a one-to-one basis. When the testing is carried out in a group setting then levels of neuroticism appear to have no bearing on the results. This has been explained by arguing that in a group setting the anxiety levels of neurotic people are not raised to the same extent as they are in a one-to-one setting. Although the research on the relationship between personality and ESP performance does appear to provide consistent results, Irwin (1999) suggests that they can be interpreted as indicating that people are most likely to demonstrate ESP when they feel comfortable and relaxed. This means that the personality tests are simply providing us with a measure of the extent to which a person is likely to feel relaxed in an experimental setting.**

## Evidence for and against ESP

Between 1964 and 1972, 15 studies were carried out at the Maimonides sleep laboratory and seven of these produced significant results. However, attempts to replicate the findings in other sleep laboratories met with little success (Beloff, 1993). Nevertheless, the dream studies were successful in popularising the free-response technique that has been used widely in parapsychological research. One of the major drawbacks of dream research is that it is extremely resource intensive and time consuming – a whole night is required for a single trial!

One of the major goals of research into ESP is to conduct an experiment that provides conclusive evidence for its existence. However, Irwin (1999) comes to the conclusion that there is and can be no single experiment that demonstrates the existence of ESP. One of the reasons he uses to support this conclusion is that there is always the possibility that one or more of the experimenters may have fraudulently altered the data in some way. It is interesting to note that this claim could be levelled at any scientific experiment. If it is not possible to demonstrate the existence of ESP through a single experiment then perhaps the only way is through the accumulation of lots of experiments that provide support for its existence. One of the techniques that enables this to be done is meta-analysis. A comprehensive meta-analysis of experiments using the autoganzfeld technique was carried out by Bem and Honorton (1994).

## Study 2.6

**AIM** Bem and Honorton (1994) aimed to carry out a meta-analysis of experiments conducted using the autoganzfeld technique.

**METHOD** Eight studies, involving a total of 100 men and 140 women, were reviewed and analysed using a meta-analytic technique.

**RESULT** When the results of the experiments were combined, the success rate of participants in identifying the correct image was significantly greater than might be expected by chance.

**CONCLUSION** The findings of the meta-analysis were taken to support the view that ESP does exist and is responsible for participants' success rate in the experiments.

One of the factors that does appear to be an important influence on the outcome of experiments investigating ESP is the social climate in the laboratory. Bem and Honorton (1994) argue that creating a friendly social climate in the laboratory is a critical factor in determining the success or failure of the experiments. Since Bem and Honorton's (1994) paper was published, further meta-analyses of experiments using the ganzfeld technique have been carried out. Milton and Wiseman (1999b) found no significant effect and concluded that the ganzfeld technique does not offer a method for reliably producing ESP in the laboratory. However, Bem, Palmer and Broughton (2001) combined the data used by Milton and Wiseman (1999b) with more recent data and again found a significant effect. There is no doubt that the debate concerning the reliability and replicability of ganzfeld experiments will continue for some time to come.

## EVALUATIVE COMMENT

One of the problems people have when it comes to evaluating their own experiences of ESP is that humans are not very good at making judgements about probability. More specifically, people are not very good at making judgements about coincidences. For example, consider an ESP experience reported by Rhine (1953). During the middle of the night a woman, who was away from home for a few days, had a strong urge to go home. When she arrived home she found the house on fire. Although this seems to be strong evidence in support of ESP it is by no means conclusive. Many people who are away from home for a period of time feel somewhat homesick and want to go home; some will actually return home. For most of them there will be nothing unexpected waiting for them but for a few there will be. In such cases their feelings about wanting to go home can be reinterpreted as a premonition or a case of clairvoyance.

# 2.4 Psychokinesis (PK)

## Methods of investigation

PK has been investigated mainly through the use of spontaneous case material and laboratory experiments. However, some interesting case studies have investigated the alleged PK powers of particular individuals. One of the problems with spontaneous case material is that instances of PK appear to occur much less frequently than ESP. Nevertheless, an impressive collection of 178 cases of spontaneously occurring PK were reported by Rhine (1963a). This provided the basis for an analysis of the characteristics of the PK experienced by people in naturalistic settings. A variety of techniques have been used to investigate PK under laboratory conditions. One of the methods that has been used extensively is dice rolling (see below). Irwin (1999) suggests that this started when a professional gambler walked into a parapsychology laboratory run by Joseph Banks Rhine in the United States and claimed that he could influence the way the dice fell.

Dice throwing is a method that has been widely used in experiments investigating PK; participants have to try and influence the numbers that are showing when the dice come to rest — a useful ability to have if you are a gambler!

## PRACTICAL activity

Imagine you are a parapsychologist investigating PK. You decide to use dice rolling to investigate whether or not members of the general public can demonstrate PK. You know that the chances of achieving a total of more than seven with two dice are 5 in 12.

**1.** Design an experiment that could be used to find out if PK exists.

**2.** Make a list of the problems associated with using dice rolling as a method of investigating and state how you would overcome them.

**3.** Now compare your design and list of problems with those of other people in your class.

One of the potential problems of using dice is that they might be biased. One of the ways in which Rhine overcame this was to have two parts to the experiment. In the first part he asked people to influence the dice so the combined total of the two dice was more than seven. In the second part he asked them to throw less than seven. In this way, if a significant result was obtained in both conditions it could not be due to biased dice. Later studies run by Rhine used a machine to roll the dice so that the participants had no physical contact with the dice at all.

More recently a technique relying on radioactive decay has been developed by Helmut Schmidt. The equipment used is called a random event generator (REG). Basically, an REG consists of a radioactive source, a counter and a visual display. The emissions from the radioactive source are responsible for stopping the counter, which in turn activates a visual display. In a typical experiment the number of different displays would be fixed – for example, seven. Which display was activated would depend on where the counter was stopped. The participant's task was to try to use PK to influence the apparatus to produce a particular display. If a display occurred significantly more frequently than chance then it could be taken as evidence for PK. The important point here is that the emissions from the radioactive source occur at random and so their effect cannot be predicted.

## EVALUATIVE COMMENT

**One of the criticisms levelled at PK studies using REGs is that although the apparatus was checked over large numbers of trials to make sure that the output was random, it was not done for the small numbers of trials that would be used in a PK experiment. If it was the case that there was a pattern to the output over relatively small numbers of trials then there is the possibility that it could have some effect on the results. However, Irwin (1999) argues that it is difficult to see how such an effect could be responsible for the actual results that have come from PK studies using REGs.**

## Types of psychokinesis

Some reported cases of psychokinesis suggest that it can occur spontaneously, but there are also reported instances of it occurring under the direct control of an individual. This would appear to suggest that it can be either a conscious or unconscious process. In PK research, a distinction is made between 'macro-PK' and 'micro-PK'. Macro-PK refers to situations where the PK has some directly observable effect, such as bending spoons or objects breaking, whereas micro-PK is concerned with situations where the effects are not directly observable but can be detected by the use of statistics. A common method used to detect micro-PK involves rolling a pair of dice. Statistics can be used to determine the likelihood of certain combinations occurring. For example, getting a score of more than seven is likely to occur by chance five times out of every twelve rolls of the dice. If an individual consistently gets a score of seven more than five times out of every twelve throws it could be used as evidence in support of PK. That is, assuming the dice are not biased in any way.

Another form of PK is referred to as direct mental interaction with living systems (DMILS) and is concerned with the potential effects of PK on living organisms. In the past this type of PK was referred to as 'bio-PK'. Many different societies have recognised that certain individuals appear to have the ability to heal others using nothing more than their touch. In parapsychology the term 'psychic healing' has been used to refer to situations where one person appears to be able to influence the physiology of another person by means not known to conventional science. One of the problems faced by anyone who attempts to investigate this phenomena experimentally is that it is very difficult to distinguish what is due to normal suggestion and what is due to the possible influence of PK (Beloff, 1993). However, if it could be shown that PK can influence human physiology then its potential would be enormous.

| Type of psychokinesis (PK) | Description |
| --- | --- |
| Macro-PK | A person can affect an object without touching it; the effect can be detected with the naked eye |
| Micro-PK | A person can affect an object without touching it; the effect can only be detected by means of a microscope or statistical analysis |
| Direct mental interaction with living systems (DMILS) | The person can influence a living organism such as another person, animal or plant |

Figure 2.14: Types of psychokinesis

## EVALUATIVE COMMENT

**Several different forms of PK have been identified in the literature ranging from bending spoons to psychic healing. The traditional view in parapsychology is that ESP and PK are separate and distinct categories of paranormal phenomena. However, Storm and Thalbourne (2000) suggest that this is not the case, and argue that it is more appropriate to consider PK and ESP as different aspects of a single paranormal process.**

## Key research: evidence for and against PK

At first sight, the evidence from spontaneous case reports appears to be quite impressive. Rhine (1963a; 1963b) came to the conclusion that the physical effects reported by the people in her cases actually occurred. There are several instances where the effects were seen by more than one person. Nearly all the cases reported by Rhine (1963a) involved two people: a person who observed the effect and a person in crisis some distance away. Rhine (1963a) found that there appeared to be a relationship between the type of crisis being experienced and the physical effect observed. The stopping and starting of clocks was associated with a person who was dying, whereas falling objects were associated with a person who was still alive.

However, one of the major criticisms of PK spontaneous case material involves the notion of chance and probability. If we consider one of the most common examples of spontaneously occurring PK, namely the stopping of clocks when someone dies, there are two possible explanations:

**1.** PK is responsible for the clock stopping

**2.** the fact that the two events occurred within a short space of time is purely coincidental; every day large numbers of people die and also clocks stop working of their own accord – this means that every now and again the two events will occur at the same time simply through chance.

One way of deciding between the two explanations would require two pieces of information. First, for any given period of time, such as a day or a week, we would need the probability of a clock stopping in a house where a close friend or relative of the occupant has died at approximately the same time. This would give us the probability of the two events occurring together by chance. Second, we would need to know how many times the two events had actually occurred together. We could then compare the number of actual occurrences with the number of occurrences that we would expect by chance. If there are significantly more occurrences than we would expect by chance then this could be used to support a paranormal explanation. However, collecting accurate information on the incidence of clocks stopping and people dying is more or less impossible. This means that establishing a causal relationship on the basis of spontaneous PK case material is extremely difficult.

The experimental work on PK has produced a number of significant findings, but the early work on dice rolling and similar techniques was subject to a considerable amount of criticism. A critique of PK was presented by Girden (1962), who examined 200 PK experiments and identified a number of flaws in all the experiments he reviewed. The flaws he identified included the possibility of recording errors, lack of control conditions and the inappropriate use of statistics. However, more recent experiments have addressed the issues raised by Girden (1962). Radin and Nelson (1989) conducted a meta-analysis of experiments using REGs and found that participants did appear to be having an effect on the REG. They concluded that, under certain circumstances, consciousness can influence physical systems. In other words, their findings provided strong evidence in support of the view that PK exists.

The majority of experimental research into DMILS has been carried out using animals or plants as the target for healing (Beloff, 1993). Some of the most convincing evidence for psychic healing comes from experiments involving Oskar Estabany, a Hungarian who emigrated to the United States. Estabany claimed to have powers of psychic healing.

**Study 2.7**

**AIM** Grad, Cadoret and Paul (1961) set out to investigate the psychic healing powers of Oskar Estabany.

**METHOD** Small skin wounds were surgically inflicted on 200 mice. The mice were randomly divided into two equal groups. The mice in one group were held by Estabany for a 15-minute period twice daily. The mice in the second group were held by different individuals each day in the same manner for the same length of time.

**RESULT** After a period of 20 days the mice in Estabany's group had significantly smaller wounds than the mice in the other group.

**CONCLUSION** The results were used to support the view that Estabany had psychic healing powers.

The results of experiments conducted with Estabany appear to have produced impressive results. However, more recent work that has investigated the effects of psychic healing on humans has been troubled by methodological problems including experimenter effects and demand characteristics. When dealing with humans it is always going to be difficult to distinguish effects that may be due to PK from effects that are due to other normal processes.

## EVALUATIVE COMMENT

**Unlike many other physical systems it would appear that the effects of PK are not cumulative. In other words, using several participants to influence a target seems to have no greater effect that using a single participant (Beloff, 1993). One of the issues in PK research, especially in spontaneous case material, is the probability of events occurring by chance. There is some evidence to suggest that people who believe in the paranormal are more likely than disbelievers to underestimate the probability of an event occurring by chance (Blackmore and Troscianko, 1985). This could explain why some people are more likely than others to consider an unusual event to be the result of paranormal activity.**

## 2.5 Sample questions

### SAMPLE QUESTION

(a)  Describe a study in which one form of psychokinesis (PK) has been investigated. Indicate in your answer the aim(s) of the study, the method used, the results obtained and conclusions drawn.
   *(AO1 = 4, AO2 = 1)*                                                                 *(5 marks)*

(b)  Evaluate the relationship between personality traits and extra-sensory perception (ESP).
   *(AO2 = 3)*                                                                          *(3 marks)*

(c)  Evaluate the evidence for and against the existence of extra-sensory perception (ESP).
   *(AO1 = 6, AO2 = 6)*                                                                *(12 marks)*

   Total AO1 marks = 10  Total AO2 marks = 10  Total = 20 marks

### QUESTIONS, ANSWERS AND COMMENTS

(a)  Describe what is meant by the term parapsychology. Refer to at least one example of paranormal experience to illustrate your answer.
   *(AO1 = 2, AO2 = 1)*                                                                 *(3 marks)*

(b)  Distinguish between demand characteristics and experimenter effects in parapsychology. Give one example of each.
   *(AO1 = 2, AO2 = 3)*                                                                 *(5 marks)*

(c)  Describe and discuss empirical evidence for the existence of psychokinesis (PK).
   *(AO1 = 6, AO2 = 6)*                                                                *(12 marks)*

   Total AO1 marks = 10  Total AO2 marks = 10  Total = 20 marks

## Answer to (a)

Parapsychology is the study of paranormal activity. 'Para' means 'beyond', so the word paranormal means 'beyond normal'. This means that parapsychology is the study of experiences and events that go beyond what we consider to be normal. It takes a scientific approach and often uses laboratory-based experiments but also makes use of information collected through case studies of individual people or events.

**Comment:** This answer would be awarded two AO1 marks but no AO2 mark. The candidate provides a satisfactory description of the term 'parapsychology' but does not refer to an example. Reference to either ESP or PK phenomena would have been sufficient to gain an AO2 mark.

## Answer to (b)

Experimenter effects in parapsychology are when the results of a study are influenced, either intentionally or unintentionally, by the researcher who is conducting the experiment. An extreme example of an experimenter effect would be if the experimenter deliberately falsified the results. Fortunately there is little evidence that this actually occurs in practice. A less extreme example of an experimenter effect is if the experimenter creates a friendly, comfortable atmosphere in the laboratory, then it is more likely to produce a significant result in an ESP experiment than if the atmosphere is less friendly. In this way the experimenter is unintentionally having an effect on the results of the experiment. Demand characteristics are when the participant guesses the nature of the experiment. This can also affect the results, because if they believe in ESP they will try and make sure the experiment is a success, but if they don't believe in ESP then they might try and make sure the experiment fails. So the difference between the two is that experimenter effects are due to the experimenter and demand characteristics are due to the participant.

**Comment:** This answer would be awarded the full 5 marks. It clearly describes each term and also elaborates on how one differs from the other. The candidate provides examples of how the two effects might operate in an experimental setting.

# Answer to (c)

Psychokinesis (PK) is concerned with the effect that a person can have on an object or living target without any physical contact. There are three basic types of PK.

1. Macro-PK, which involves effects that can be seen with the naked eye. A popular example was the spoon bending done by Uri Geller in the 1970s. There are also spontaneous macro-PK events, such as reports of clocks stopping when someone dies.

2. Micro-PK is concerned with the effects of PK that can only be noticed microscopically or by the use of statistical analyses. A typical example involves affecting the numbers that are face up when a pair of dice are rolled.

3. Direct mental interaction with living systems (DMILS). This involves PK being used to influence a living thing such as a person, an animal or a plant.

Evidence for the existence of macro-PK comes mainly from the use of case studies. Case studies have been used in two ways. First, large numbers of reports of spontaneous occurrences of PK have been collected and analysed. This was done by Rhine (1963a) and it provided useful information about the types of macro-PK experienced by people. One of the main problems with this type of research is that it relies on the subjective reports of individuals and it takes little account of the likelihood of events occurring by chance; for example, on occasions clocks stop working on their own, and every day large numbers of people die. This means that there is a probability of the two events occurring at the same time just by chance. Uri Geller performed spoon bending on television but was unwilling to go into a laboratory to demonstrate his ability under carefully controlled conditions. So there is very little conclusive evidence that can be used to argue for the existence of macro-PK. Micro-PK effects have been investigated using the dice-rolling method. Participants have to try and influence the numbers that are face up when a pair of dice are rolled. Because the probability of scores occurring by chance can be calculated it means that a participant's performance can be compared to what you would expect them to get by chance. A meta-analysis carried out by Radin and Ferrari (1991) of dice-throwing studies showed a significant difference between the experimental and control conditions. In other words, it provided evidence of the existence of micro-PK. But one of the problems with meta-analysis is that you don't know how many experiments have been carried out and found no significant results. There is a tendency for journals only to publish papers that have found a significant difference between conditions. This means that the meta-analysis is only being carried out on experiments that found a significant effect, which would bias the results. This bias is sometimes referred to as the 'file-drawer effect' because the results of non-significant experiments are often left in the drawer of a filing cabinet. One of the ways that research in parapsychology has tried to avoid the file-drawer problem is to encourage researchers to publish the results of all their experiments whether they are significant or not.

Another type of PK that has provided positive evidence of its existence is where a person attempts to interact directly with another person or animal. This is called direct mental interaction with living systems (DMILS). One study was reported by Grad, Cadoret and Paul (1961), who set out to investigate the psychic healing powers of Oskar Estabany. In this study small cuts were put into the skin of mice. Estabany held some of the mice for a short time every day; someone else held the other mice for the same length of time each day. The cuts on the mice held by Estabany were significantly smaller than the cuts in the other mice. This was taken to support the view that DMILS exists. But one of the problems that arises when investigating the DMILS effects on humans rather than animals is that it is always going to be difficult to distinguish effects that may be due to PK from effects that are due to other normal processes.

**Comment:** This is a very good answer and would probably be awarded the full 12 marks. It starts off with a clear description of the different types of PK. Then it presents evidence in support of the existence of PK, but also highlights some of the problems associated with the research. It mentions the dice-throwing studies and the meta-analysis carried out by Radin and Ferrari (1991). Perhaps there could have been some reference to the REG studies that have been the focus of micro-PK research in recent years. One final point: it is important to bear in mind that when answering this question no credit would be awarded for any reference to ESP, the question is only concerned with evidence that supports the existence of PK.

# 2.6 FURTHER READING

Introductory texts

Blackmore, S.J. 1996: **In Search of the Light: The Adventures of a Parapsychologist**. Prometheus Books, Amherst NY

Kane, B., Millay, J. & Brown, D.H. (eds) 1993: **Silver Threads: Twenty-five Years of Parapsychology Research**. Praeger Publishers/Greenwood Publishing Group, Inc., Westport CT

## Specialist sources

Beloff, J. 1993: **Parapsychology: A Concise History**. Athlone Press, London

Irwin, H.J. 1999: **An Introduction to Parapsychology**. 3rd Ed. McFarland, London

Roberts, R. & Groome, D. (eds) 2001: **Parapsychology: The Psychology of Unusual Experience**. Arnold, London

# 3

# Substance abuse

## 3.1 Use and abuse

The terms 'use' and 'abuse' are often used in this area and it is important to distinguish between them. Like many of the terms associated with substance abuse there is no single definition that is universally accepted. Generally speaking, 'substance use' refers to situations in which people are not in danger of any immediate harm from the substance they are taking. On the other

| Term | Definition |
|------|------------|
| Substance use | The use of a substance without any immediate harm to the person |
| Substance misuse | The use of a substance in a way that results in the person experiencing social, psychological, physical or legal problems |
| Substance abuse | The use of a substance in a way that causes harm |

Figure 3.1: Definitions of some common terms (adapted from Drugscope, 2001)

hand, 'substance abuse' refers to situations where a person will experience some form of harm as a consequence of using the substance (although it has been argued that the term 'abuse' is rather judgemental because it implies some form of wrongdoing regardless of how the substance is being used). In many situations the term 'misuse' is used as an alternative to 'abuse' (Drugscope, 2001).

The harmful consequences of substance abuse can be placed into four categories. The first concerns a failure to fulfil important obligations at work, home or school. This would include behaviours such as being late, and not turning up for meetings. The second category is concerned with repeatedly using the substance in dangerous situations – for example, when driving a car or swimming. Third, the person has repeated problems involving the legal system and is frequently arrested for a variety of offences. The fourth category is concerned with the social problems that arise as a result of the substance abuse, and includes problems with family and friends.

## EVALUATIVE COMMENT

**When considering the use and abuse of substances it is important to bear in mind the fact that different societies have different views and laws. For example, in some countries buying, selling and drinking alcohol is illegal. In the United Kingdom it is not illegal to buy alcohol, provided you are over the age of 18, but there are laws governing who can sell it, and when and where it can be sold. In this country attitudes towards the use and abuse of alcohol and other substances have changed over time.**

## Distinction between addiction and dependence

Distinguishing between 'addiction' and 'dependence' is not an easy task because there is no universally agreed upon definition of either term. It is certainly the case that definitions in this area are continually being revised in the light of new information (Maddux, 2000). A recent definition of addiction states that addiction is a 'behaviour over which an individual has impaired control with harmful consequences' (West, 2001). In other words, individuals recognise that their behaviour is harming them or others that they care about, but they are unable to stop it.

One way of distinguishing between the two terms is to look at the effects that psychoactive substances have on the brain. A psychoactive substance is one that affects a person's mood and behaviour by acting on the neurotransmitters in the brain (Pinel, 2003). Broadly speaking, addictive behaviour is associated with the reward centres in the brain. An addictive behaviour is one in which the person is seeking to stimulate the reward centres of the brain. The chemicals in the brain responsible for transmitting information from one neuron (brain cell) to another are called neurotransmitters. Dopamine is a neurotransmitter that has been associated with most, if not all, addictive behaviours.

Olds and Milner (1954) were the first researchers to explore the role of specific areas of the brain in maintaining certain behaviours. They implanted electrodes in the brains of rats, which supplied a small electric current when the rat pressed a lever. When animals are able to give themselves electrical brain stimulation it is referred to as 'self-stimulation'. Olds and Milner (1954) found that the rats pressed the lever very frequently, indicating that they found the self-stimulation a pleasant experience. (There are even some reports of the rats continuing to press the lever until they are too exhausted to continue.) More recent research has indicated that self-stimulation results in an increase in the levels of dopamine in the brain (Phillips *et al.*, 1992). This suggests that dopamine is the neurotransmitter that is associated with our feelings of pleasure and excitement. In terms of substance abuse the interesting point is that all the substances that are abused appear to cause an increase in the level of dopamine in the brain (Carlson, 1993). So addiction has its basis in the rewarding and pleasurable experience associated with the use of a psychoactive substance. However, not everyone who uses a psychoactive substance can be considered to be an addict. One of the important aspects of any definition of addiction is the notion that people who are addicted continue to use a substance even though it is having an adverse effect on their health and social life.

If a person takes a psychoactive substance for a prolonged period of time, their body and in particular their neurons adapt and alter the way in which they operate. In other words, the presence of the psychoactive substance in their body becomes the 'normal' state. When this happens we can say that the person has become physically dependent on the substance. If the levels of the psychoactive substance in the body begin to decrease it is usually an unpleasant experience for the person concerned. So in contrast to addiction, which is associated with bringing about a pleasant experience, dependence is concerned with avoiding an unpleasant state.

| Addiction | Dependence |
|---|---|
| Addiction refers to the seeking out of activities that are pleasurable even though they are having an adverse effect on a person's health and social life | Dependence comes about when the body needs a substance to bring it back to a 'normal' state; in other words, it is concerned with avoiding an unpleasant state |

Figure 3.2: The distinction between addiction and dependence

Dependence describes a compulsion to continue taking a drug in order to feel good or to avoid feeling bad (Drugscope, 2001). There are two types of dependence: physical dependence and psychological dependence. At one time physical dependence was seen as the main reason for a person's addiction to a substance. It was thought that people continued using a substance to avoid the withdrawal symptoms that developed if they stopped taking it. However, if this was the case then it should be relatively straightforward to 'cure' people who are addicted to a substance. It would seem to suggest that once people have overcome the physical effects of stopping using a substance they will no longer want to use it. This is clearly not the case since many people return to substance abuse long after the physical withdrawal symptoms have ceased.

A person who suffers an addiction is often referred to as an addict; however, it is becoming increasingly common to use the term 'problem drug user' instead; one of the problems with words like 'addiction' and 'addict' is that they are often used in a very judgemental way

## PRACTICAL Activity

Think about the word 'addict'. Make a list of the characteristics you think are associated with someone who is an addict. For each characteristic on your list ask yourself what evidence you have to support your view.

Traditionally addiction has been considered in relation to drug use. However, an alternative approach sees addiction in a much broader sense. Griffiths (1995) argues that people can develop addictive behaviours for a wide range of activities, and sees addiction to drugs as only one possibility. For example, it would appear that people can become addicted to gambling. Griffiths (1995) argues that addictive behaviours have six components:

1. importance of the activity in a person's life – addictive behaviours become the most important activity in a person's life

2. the experience of carrying out the addictive behaviour – the addictive behaviour is associated with a 'rush' of excitement, or some sort of emotional 'high'

3. tolerance – typically, an addict has to increase the level of the behaviour to get the same effect

4. withdrawal symptoms – when the addictive behaviour is stopped the person experiences unpleasant physical sensations and emotions

**5.** conflict – people with addictive behaviours have a negative effect on the people around them, such as friends and family; this can lead to arguments and conflict

**6.** relapse – although some people manage to stop their addictive behaviours there is always a relatively high risk of relapse.

## EVALUATIVE COMMENT

**The British Medical Association (BMA) suggests that it is becoming increasingly common for medical experts to avoid using the term 'addiction' (BMA, 1997). One main reason behind an avoidance of the word addiction is that it is closely tied in to society's views about substance abuse and the people who abuse substances. These views are invariably negative, which means that being described as an addict is often seen as an insult. It is becoming increasingly common to use the term 'problem drug user' instead of addict. Griffiths' (1995) approach to addiction is helpful because it enables us to consider addictive behaviours within a broader psychological framework. It also has the advantage of enabling us to look at the similarities between different forms of addictive behaviour.**

## 3.2 Types of abuse and substances

The use of substances such as cocaine, nicotine and alcohol for non-medical reasons has been the focus of a considerable amount of psychological research. Some of these substances are often referred to as 'drugs' (e.g. cocaine) but it is becoming increasingly common to use the term 'substance'. One of the reasons for this is that some substances, such as alcohol and nicotine, are widely used and are not normally thought of as drugs by the general public. Nolen-Hoeksema (2001) argues that the term 'substance' is more neutral than the term 'drug' because it is less likely to be used in a judgemental way.

### Psychological dependence, tolerance and withdrawal

Physical dependence develops when the body's chemistry changes so that it needs the presence of a substance to function normally. If the levels of the substance become lowered because the person has not been using it, then they will normally experience unpleasant withdrawal symptoms. Psychological dependence refers to a situation where a person's life has become centred around substance abuse. The substance abuse becomes their main topic of conversation and their daily activities are structured to enable them to use the substance. They have reached a state where they have come to rely on the substance to enable them to feel good. The feelings will be dependent on the particular substance being abused but they typically include feelings of relaxation or self-confidence, or feeling full of energy.

If a person uses a substance for a period of time their body begins to adapt to it. This means that they require more of the substance in order to achieve the same effect. This is referred to as 'tolerance'. For example, when a person first starts drinking alcohol they only require a relatively small amount before they start to feel the effect. But if they continue drinking over a period of years their bodies become tolerant to alcohol and they need to drink a lot more before they notice any effect. However, at some point these effects level off (Sarafino, 1990). Tolerance to a particular substance can be shown in two ways: first, by showing that a specific amount of the substance has less effect than it had before the person started using the substance; second, by showing that it takes more of the substance to produce the same effect (Pinel, 2003).

It is quite common for people who abuse heroin to die as the result of an overdose. Many of these deaths can be attributed to factors such as mixing heroin with other substances or using heroin from a different supply. However, in some cases people have died as a result of taking the same dose of heroin, from the same source, as they had taken the previous day. The only difference was that the 'overdose' had been taken in a place that the person was not familiar with. This would seem to suggest that the setting in which a substance is used can have an effect on the tolerance levels of an individual. In other words, tolerance to a substance such as heroin can be conditioned to the environment in which the drug is normally used. This form of tolerance is referred to as 'conditioned drug tolerance'.

**Study 3.1**

**AIM** Siegel *et al.* (1982) set out to investigate the extent to which drug tolerance is dependent on the situation.

**METHOD** Rats were administered heroin in their normal living quarters for a period of 30 days. This allowed the rats to develop a tolerance to heroin. Then the rats were given a potentially lethal dose of heroin. One group was given the injection in their normal living quarters, the other group was given the injection in a new environment that they had not experienced before.

**RESULT** Approximately 65 per cent of the rats that were given the potentially lethal injection in the new environment died. Whereas only 30 per cent of the rats that were given the injection in the setting where they had previously been injected died.

**CONCLUSION** The findings were taken as strong support for the view that drug tolerance can be conditioned to the environment.

Siegel *et al.* (1982) argued that classical conditioning is responsible for the way in which drug tolerance can become associated with particular settings. A simplified account of the way in which classical conditioning occurs is presented in Figure 3.4. Each time the person uses a substance is considered to be a classical conditioning trial.

The environmental features of the setting where the substance is normally used, such as the room and other people present, is considered to be the conditional stimulus (CS). Taking the substance is the unconditioned stimulus (UCS) and the level of tolerance to the substance is the

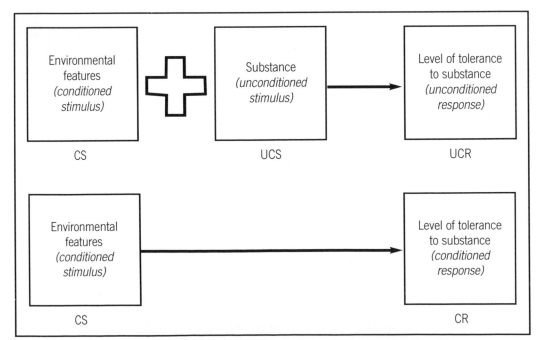

Figure 3.4: Simplified representation of Siegel *et al.*'s (1982) theory of conditioned drug tolerance

unconditioned response (UCR). After a number of 'trials', or occasions when the substance has been used, the environmental features become associated with the level of tolerance to the substance, which in turn becomes the conditioned response (CR). This would mean that the level of tolerance to a substance is affected by the environment within which the substance is taken. In other words, a person's tolerance level would decrease if they take the substance in a different environment. If Siegel *et al.* (1982) are correct then it could account for some of the unexplained 'overdose' deaths where people have taken their normal dose in a strange environment.

When a person stops using a substance they have been using for a while this can result in 'withdrawal effects'. Withdrawal effects are typically the opposite to the initial effect of the substance. This is because withdrawal symptoms are the body's way of compensating for the absence of a particular substance. This means that if a substance produces a relaxing effect when it is first used, say, then the withdrawal effect would be anxiety (see Figure 3.5).

| Effects of heroin | Heroin withdrawal symptoms |
|---|---|
| Feeling elated and happy | Feeling down and unhappy |
| Constipation | Diarrhoea and stomach cramps |
| Feeling relaxed | Feeling agitated |

Figure 3.5: The effects and withdrawal symptoms of heroin

The nature of withdrawal symptoms depends on a number of factors, including the particular substance being abused, the level of abuse, and whether stopping using the drug occurs immediately or is a more gradual process.

## EVALUATIVE COMMENT

**Not all substances have the same risk of tolerance. For example, people can develop a tolerance to alcohol, nicotine and stimulants, but are less likely to develop a tolerance to cannabis. It was once thought that physical dependency was the main cause of addiction. Psychological dependence was seen as the cause of addictions to substances that do not result in physical dependence. However, more recently the term 'dependence' has been used to include both psychological and physical dependence. One of the reasons behind this is that it is now fairly clear that physical dependence is not the main cause of addictive behaviour. So there seems little use in maintaining a distinction between psychological and physical dependence (Pinel, 2003).**

## Solvent abuse

Solvents have many uses and can be found in glues, paints, nail varnish removers, aerosols and cigarette lighters. Many solvents give off a vapour at room temperature, which can be inhaled and which produces effects similar to alcohol. Recent figures suggest that as many as 21 per cent of 15–16 year olds say they have tried solvents (Drugscope, 2001). Perhaps one of the reasons for their widespread use is that solvents are cheap and easy to purchase. The experience of inhaling solvents is similar to being drunk on alcohol. People tend to feel dizzy and experience a sense of unreality.

**Study 3.2**

**AIM** Field-Smith *et al.* (2002) set out to investigate recent trends in the number of deaths in the United Kingdom from solvent abuse.

**METHOD** Data was collected from a number of sources, including HM Coroners and the press for the period 1971–2000.

**RESULT** The number of deaths from solvent abuse in the UK reached a peak of 152 in 1990. Since then, there has been a significant decrease in the number of deaths. In 2000 there were 64 deaths associated with solvent abuse.

**CONCLUSION** In 1992 the Department of Health was responsible for an advertising campaign aimed at parents. The decrease in the number of deaths is taken as support for the effectiveness of the campaign.

Research has indicated that solvent abuse is equally common in both males and females (Chadwick *et al.*, 1991) and a recent survey reported that 7 per cent of secondary school boys and 8 per cent of secondary school girls had misused solvents in 2001 (DoH, 2002). Despite the fact that there seem to be equal numbers of boys and girls misusing solvents, significantly more males die as a result than females. If we just consider people under the age of 18, then in the period 1983–2000 males accounted for approximately 80 per cent of the deaths associated with solvent abuse (Field-Smith *et al.*, 2002).

The component of tobacco that is responsible for causing dependency is nicotine; nicotine is absorbed into the bloodstream very quickly and its effects are noticed almost immediately; however, it is also the case that nicotine levels in the body decline relatively quickly too – it takes about 30 minutes for the nicotine levels in a person's body to decline by 50 per cent

## Tobacco and nicotine

Tobacco leaves contain a mild stimulant called nicotine, which turns into a vapour when the dried leaves are burnt. The nicotine in cigarette smoke, along with other substances such as carbon monoxide (a poisonous gas), are absorbed into the body by the lungs. There are many different tobacco products, such as cigarettes, cigars and pipe tobacco, which contain dried tobacco leaves. Since tobacco was first brought into the UK in the late sixteenth century, the tobacco industry has developed into a multi-billion-pound enterprise. Although it is illegal to sell tobacco products to anyone under the age of 16 there are very few convictions of people doing so. For example, in the UK in 1999 there were only 136 convictions for selling tobacco to under-16s (Drugscope, 2001). There is little doubt now about the health risks associated with smoking. It has been estimated that, worldwide, tobacco products are responsible for three million deaths a year and this number continues to rise (World Health Organization, 1997).

Tomkins (1968) proposed that there are four different types of smoking behaviour: habitual, positive emotion, negative emotion, and addictive (see Figure 3.7). According to Tomkins (1968) habitual smokers are not really aware of their smoking but continue to smoke because it has become a routine or habit. In contrast, addictive smokers are very aware of when they are smoking and not smoking. It is quite likely that they will be able to tell you exactly how long it is since their last cigarette. Positive emotion smokers do so because they want to increase their feelings of relaxation and other positive emotions, whereas negative emotion smokers are trying to reduce their levels of anxiety and stress.

| Type of smoker | Description |
|---|---|
| Habitual | Continues smoking as a matter of habit; they derive little pleasure from the activity and are often unaware that they are smoking |
| Positive emotion | Smoking provides a way of relaxing and feeling good |
| Negative emotion | Smoking provides a way of reducing anxiety and stress |
| Addictive | Are aware of their smoking and are also aware of the times when they are not smoking |

Figure 3.7: Tomkins' (1968) types of smoker

A number of factors have been identified that appear to be associated with the decision to start smoking. According to Stead *et al.* (1996), these can be organised into three broad categories:

1. personal factors, such as beliefs about the consequences of smoking

2. sociocultural factors, including the influence of family and friends

3. environmental factors, such as the cost and availability of cigarettes.

The influence of 'significant others' such as friends, family and peers on smoking behaviour has been recognised by many researchers (Frankland, 1998). Secondary school pupils who smoke seem to associate with other children who smoke (Diamond and Goddard, 1995). Traditionally, this apparent relationship has been explained in terms of peer-group pressure – in other words, children who smoke try to persuade others to smoke as well. However, this view has been challenged by Mitchell (1997), who found little evidence of peer pressure influencing whether or not people smoke. It seems to be the case that adolescents who want to smoke are active in seeking situations where this is possible, whereas those who do not avoid situations where people are smoking.

## Alcohol

Estimates suggest that over 90 per cent of the adult population in the UK have consumed alcohol at some point in their lives. Despite the fact that the legal age for purchasing alcohol in the UK is 18, it has been estimated that approximately 60 per cent of children aged between 13 and 17 have bought alcohol (Drugscope, 2001). Alcoholic drinks contain ethyl alcohol (or ethanol), which is responsible for their effect. Alcohol is classified as a depressant because at moderate to high doses it reduces neurotransmitter activity in the brain. However, at relatively low doses alcohol can have the opposite effect and act as a stimulant. Alcohol is absorbed into the bloodstream and normally starts to have an effect on the body within ten minutes. People develop a tolerance to alcohol, which means that its effects will depend on how much the person is used to drinking (Drugscope, 2001).

Alcohol is also capable of producing physical dependence and can give rise to severe withdrawal symptoms (Nolen-Hoeksema, 2001). Winger *et al.* (1992) have proposed a three-stage model of withdrawal from alcohol dependence (see Figure 3.8). The first stage usually begins a few hours after the last drink. The person will shake, sweat, and occasionally be sick and have stomach cramps. The second stage normally occurs on the second or third day after the person has stopped drinking. It involves convulsions or seizures. The third stage is characterised by the person experiencing hallucinations, which are referred to as *delirium tremens* (DTs). The hallucinations can be very frightening and often extremely bizarre. Approximately 11 per cent of people who experience withdrawal symptoms will have seizures or DTs and, of these, 10 per cent will die (Schuckit *et al.*, 1995). Whether or not the person experiences the second and third stages depends on the level of their alcohol dependence. If the dependence is moderate then a person may only experience the first stage. People who experience the second and third stages are those who have drunk extremely heavily for long periods of time.

| Stage | Symptoms |
|---|---|
| 1 | Shaking, sweating, feelings of anxiety, nausea and stomach cramps |
| 2 | Convulsions and seizures |
| 3 | Hallucinations (DTs), fever and irregular heart beat may develop |

Figure 3.8: Summary of the Winger *et al.* (1992) three-stage model of withdrawal from alcohol dependence

The short-term effects of alcohol depend on a variety of factors. Some people appear to become relaxed and happy when they have consumed a moderate amount of alcohol, but approximately 30 per cent of people become aggressive (Taylor and Leonard, 1983). It would appear that the relationship between alcohol and aggression is not simple or straightforward. Brannon and Feist (1992) suggest that alcohol-related aggression is behaviour that may occur in certain situations with certain individuals. In other words, whether or not a person who consumes alcohol becomes aggressive depends on their personal characteristics and the situation they are in.

Long-term alcohol abuse is associated with a type of brain damage referred to as Korsakoff's syndrome. This is a memory disorder that is common in people who are long-term, heavy users of alcohol. People suffering from Korsakoff's syndrome have great difficulty in retaining information about recent events and an inability to learn new things. Typically Korsakoff's syndrome is a progressive disease and eventually people's memory of childhood events becomes affected as well (Pinel, 2003).

## EVALUATIVE COMMENT

**There is evidence that people who abuse alcohol can be categorised into different sub-types. For example, Zucker *et al.* (1996) make a distinction on the basis of personality. They propose that some alcoholics have antisocial personalities whereas others do not. Antisocial alcohol abusers tend to find it more difficult to stop or reduce their alcohol intake, and are also more likely to be involved in other forms of substance abuse than non-antisocial alcohol abusers.**

## Stimulants

'Stimulants' are substances that stimulate the central nervous system. When used they typically result in feelings of happiness, and the user will feel full of energy. Common stimulants include amphetamines, cocaine, caffeine and alkyl nitrites. Of these, cocaine and amphetamines are most commonly associated with substance abuse. Cocaine comes from the leaves of the coca plant and when taken typically produces feelings of exhilaration, self-confidence and well-being. The psychological and physiological effects resulting from the use of cocaine are fairly short-lived. When sniffed, the effects peak after about

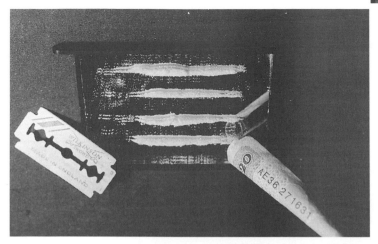

Approximately 9 per cent of people aged 20 to 24 report having used cocaine at some point in their lives

20 minutes, which means that the dose has to be repeated to maintain the effect (Drugscope, 2001). People do not develop a tolerance to cocaine and the withdrawal effects are not as severe as with other substances, such as alcohol and heroin. However, people do develop a dependence on cocaine. Cocaine dependence is characterised by a cycle of heavy use (cocaine sprees) followed by a period of recovery. During the recovery period individuals will often use other substances, such as alcohol or cannabis, to relax (Caan, 2002). Caan (2002) points out that although people dependent on cocaine may find it relatively easy to stop taking it, the risk of relapse is very high. Relative to other substances cocaine is quite expensive, which means that its use is rather limited (Drugscope, 2001).

Amphetamines are a major group of stimulants and they have a variety of street names including 'uppers', 'speed' and 'whizz'. The effect of taking amphetamines is similar to that of cocaine, but rather longer lasting, with the effects of a single dose typically lasting about four hours. As well as having an effect on a person's mood amphetamines also produce physical effects, such as slower heart rate, and increased blood supply to the muscles. Tolerance to amphetamines develops quite rapidly, so more and more of the substance is needed to produce the desired effect. A common pattern with amphetamine abusers is a cycle of heavy use followed by a period of exhaustion and depression (Davison and Neale, 2001). Amphetamines seem to increase the levels of the neurotransmitter dopamine in the parts of the brain associated with pleasure.

Ecstasy (or MDMA) is a type of amphetamine known as a hallucinogenic amphetamine. It is usually taken in the form of a pill and its effects are experienced after about 30 to 60 minutes. The psychological effects of ecstasy are typically feelings of calmness and friendliness towards other people. At moderate levels of ecstasy intake people can experience hallucinations. Since 1990 in the UK there have been approximately 100 deaths that are directly associated with taking ecstasy.

## EVALUATIVE COMMENT

**Stimulants do not have the same effect on everyone. An individual's existing psychological traits are likely to determine the way in which they experience particular stimulants (Caan, 2002). There is some indication that amphetamine abuse in the UK is on the decrease whereas cocaine and ecstasy abuse is increasing.**

## Depressants

Depressants slow down the activity of the central nervous system; in other words, they have the opposite effect to the stimulants discussed above. People taking low doses of depressants tend to feel calm and relaxed, but high doses can result in the person becoming unconscious. There are quite a few substances that are classified as depressants (see Figure 3.10). Alcohol and solvent abuse have been discussed above so this section will focus on the most commonly used opiate (heroin) and tranquillisers.

| Drug group | Commonly abused substances |
|---|---|
| Opiates (narcotics) | Heroin |
| Alcohol | Beer; spirits (whisky, vodka) |
| Solvents | Glue; lighter fuel |
| Tranquillisers (benzodiazapines) | Diazepam (valium); temazepam |

Figure 3.10: Commonly abused depressants

Heroin is one of a group of drugs called 'opiates', which are derived from the poppy plant. Heroin can be taken in a number of ways, including smoking and injecting into the veins. Heroin produces both tolerance and dependence very quickly. One of the features of heroin and other opiates is that once tolerance has developed it reaches a point where the positive effects of the drug are no longer evident. People have to take the drug just to feel 'normal' (Drugscope, 2001). Withdrawal symptoms usually last for about seven days but are considerably less dangerous than withdrawal from alcohol. The standard view is that repeated use of heroin automatically leads to long-term addiction (Bootzin *et al.*, 1993). However, the experience of American soldiers serving in the Vietnam War during the 1960s has given rise to an alternative view. During the war in Vietnam many soldiers used heroin as a means of coping with the stressful situation they found themselves in, and consequently developed a heroin dependence. However, most of them stopped using heroin when they returned home (Bourne, 1974). This has led to the view that in some situations heroin abuse can be seen as means of coping with the stressful events that people have to face in their lives. If these stresses are removed then the majority of people appear to be able to stop using heroin (Bootzin *et al.*, 1993).

Tranquillisers have been routinely prescribed by GPs in the UK for the past 20 years. Unlike some of the other substances that are abused (e.g. heroin), tranquillisers do not appear to be manufactured illegally. Tranquilliser abuse is based on drugs that have been acquired legally using a prescription or by theft from a chemist or some other source (Drugscope, 2001). The abuse of one group of tranquillisers, benzodiazepines, is a growing problem in the UK. Although the pattern of benzodiazepine abuse changes over time, it would appear that at present temazepam is the preferred substance in the UK (Ashton, 2002). Benzodiazepines can be taken in a number of ways: they can be inhaled through the nose, injected or taken orally in tablet form. Benzodiazepines are typically abused in combination with some other substance or substances. This is called 'polysubstance abuse' and refers to situations where people have become dependent on more than one substance. It is common for people who abuse alcohol to also abuse benzodiazepines. One of the reasons given for people who abuse benzodiazepines is that their use seems to enhance the effect of other substances, such as heroin (Ashton, 2002). Regular use of benzodiazepines results in dependence and withdrawal symptoms. Seivewright and Dougal (1993) identified a number of symptoms that occurred during the withdrawal from benzodiazepine abuse, including depression, shaking, nausea, dizziness and hallucinations.

## EVALUATIVE COMMENT

**The extent to which an individual can become addicted to temazepam is highlighted by a case described by Parrot (1995). The person had resorted to injecting temazepam into his groin area because the veins in his arms had become damaged as a consequence of repeated injections. The injections in his groin resulted in medical problems that meant he had to have one of his legs amputated. Some time later he was re-admitted to hospital because he had continued injecting into his remaining leg. This leg was also amputated as a result of the temazepam abuse. After a prolonged period of heroin abuse many of the positive effects are no longer experienced. However, a feeling of 'safety' and immunity from life's stresses does seem to be an effect that remains constant. Continued heroin abuse seems to be maintained to a large extent by individuals' attempts to avoid negative emotions (Caan, 2002).**

# 3.3 Psychological characteristics of abuse

## Why people abuse substances

Substance abuse is more likely to occur during adolescence than at any other time in a person's life. There is also some evidence to suggest that the younger a person is when they first start abusing a substance the higher the risk there is of them continuing to abuse it (Sarafino, 1990). However, the reasons why people abuse substances are extremely complex. The BMA (1997) has identified eight factors that appear to have some influence on whether or not people abuse substances. The factors are: personality and mental illness, genetics, family environment, peer pressure, socioeconomic factors, pleasure, availability and advertising, and finally the price of the substance.

## PRACTICAL Activity

Speak to someone you know who smokes. Ask them the following questions.

**1.** How many cigarettes do you smoke in a typical day?

**2.** How did you start smoking?

**3.** Why do you continue to smoke?

**4.** Have you ever tried to stop smoking? (If they have tried, and failed, ask them why they were not successful.)

If you are doing this as part of a class exercise you might find it interesting to compare your answers with the answers of other members of the class. Look in particular at the reasons people give for continuing to smoke. How do the reasons that people give compare with the factors identified by the BMA that are associated with substance abuse?

It is possible to identify three quite different theoretical approaches that have attempted to explain why people abuse substances. These are the biopsychological approach, the social learning approach and operant conditioning. Each of these is briefly described below.

## BIOPSYCHOLOGICAL THEORIES OF SUBSTANCE ABUSE

Pinel (2003) identifies two quite different biopsychological theories that attempt to explain why people abuse substances. The first theory tries to explain substance abuse in terms of physical dependence. According to this theory an individual continues to abuse a substance in order to avoid withdrawal symptoms. If this theory is correct, then once a person is no longer experiencing any withdrawal symptoms they should be in a position to stop their substance abuse. This view led to the development of treatment programmes that aimed to help people cope with their withdrawal symptoms. However, these approaches have typically failed and people return to a pattern of substance abuse. The physical dependence theory of substance abuse has been developed in order to account for the way in which people tend to return to substance abuse after they have overcome the withdrawal symptoms. It has been suggested that conditioning can account for the fact that people frequently relapse when they return to a situation where they have previously engaged in substance abuse, although there is little evidence to support the conditioning explanation of relapse (Pinel, 2003).

The second biopsychological theory of substance abuse proposes that people abuse substances because of the positive effects they experience. This is referred to as the 'positive-incentive' (or 'pleasure-producing') theory (Pinel, 2003). The theory recognises that in some situations people abuse substances to escape from some unpleasant aspects of their life, but it argues that the main reason why people abuse substances is because of the pleasure they experience (Stewart *et al.*, 1984). However, this theory has problems coping with the fact that people develop a tolerance to some substances – for example, heroin – to the extent that taking it is no longer a pleasurable experience. A person eventually reaches a state where using heroin merely alleviates any withdrawal symptoms and is no longer a pleasurable experience.

## SOCIAL LEARNING THEORY APPROACH TO SUBSTANCE ABUSE

Sociocultural factors appear to play a more significant role in some forms of substance abuse than others. For example, it has been argued that the main reasons why people start to drink alcohol involve sociocultural factors (Sarafino, 1990). It is quite common for adolescents to see other people who are drinking having a good time (this observation may be made through the media, or through friends and family members). The social learning processes (Bandura, 1986) result in adolescents acquiring expectancies about the positive effects of alcohol. In other words, adolescents begin to see drinking alcohol as a positive, sociable and 'grown-up' experience.

According to social learning theory one of the ways in which we learn how to behave is through the observation of other people; if young people perceive getting drunk as an enjoyable experience then they are more likely to do it themselves

## OPERANT CONDITIONING AND SUBSTANCE ABUSE

Operant conditioning has been used as another explanation for substance abuse. Davidson (1985) has argued that people's drinking behaviour can be maintained or increased through either positive or negative reinforcement. Positive re-inforcement can occur if people enjoy the effect that taking the substance has on them. There are two types of effect that can be responsible for positive reinforcement. The first is the physical and psychological sensations that arise as a direct consequence of using the substance. For example, some people like the taste of alcohol, then there is the 'high' that people experience when they use cocaine, or the feelings of relaxation that heroin users report;

these are all experiences that are likely to provide positive reinforcement. The second source of positive reinforcement is concerned with the effect that some substances have on a person's ability to feel relaxed in social situations. For example, one of the effects of alcohol is that it makes people feel less inhibited, which in turn can enable them to behave differently in social situations. If people see this as having a positive effect on their ability to form relationships this could also serve as a form of positive reinforcement. In the case of negative reinforcement, substance abuse can be one way of removing some negative features of a person's life (Adesso, 1985). For example, many heroin abusers report that one of the main attractions of heroin is that it stops them feeling bad about their lives.

## EVALUATIVE COMMENT

**Easthope (1993) presents evidence which suggests that there is still little agreement about the extent to which we can explain substance abuse in terms of a single cause or whether we should be looking for multiple causes. One of the implications of this disagreement is that it gives rise to different views about the appropriate ways of preventing substance abuse and treating people who abuse substances. Robinson and Berridge (2000) have developed a positive-incentive theory of substance abuse. Their theory argues that it is not the pleasure that comes from the actual substance abuse itself that is important, but rather it is the anticipation of taking the substance that is responsible for the positive-incentive effect. This version of the positive-incentive theory is capable of coping with the fact that people continue to abuse substances even when they derive little pleasure from the effects of the substance itself.**

## Hereditary factors and personality characteristics of alcohol abusers

There is considerable evidence that alcohol abuse runs in families. For example, Peters and Preedy (2002) suggest that approximately half the people who abuse alcohol have a close relative who is also an alcohol abuser. On the face of it this would seem to point to a hereditary link in terms of alcohol abuse. However, the fact that alcohol abuse runs in families could also be explained in terms of social learning theory. Children see their parents and other family members abusing alcohol, and see it as an adult behaviour they would like to copy. Evidence in support of the view that some people have a genetic predisposition to alcohol abuse has been found in research which has demonstrated that it is possible to breed animals that prefer alcohol to other drinks (Li and McBride, 1995).

Strong evidence for the view that alcohol abuse has a hereditary basis comes from twin studies. The rationale behind twin studies is that monozygotic (identical) twins have identical genes, whereas dizygotic (fraternal) twins do not. If there is a hereditary basis to alcohol abuse then we would expect identical twins to be more similar in their levels of alcohol abuse than non-identical twins.

**Study 3.3**

**AIM** McGue *et al.* (1992) carried out an investigation into the level of alcohol abuse in twins.

**METHOD** The level of alcohol abuse was identified in identical and fraternal twins.

**RESULT** The level of alcohol abuse was more similar in identical twins than in fraternal twins.

**CONCLUSION** The findings were taken to support the view that alcohol abuse has a hereditary component.

Further evidence for the hereditability of alcohol abuse comes from adoption studies. One of the strategies in adoption studies is to compare adopted children who have a parent who is an alcohol abuser with adopted children whose parents do not abuse alcohol. The adopted children grew up in homes where there was no evidence of alcohol abuse. Research suggests that approximately 18 per cent of adoptees with a parent who abused alcohol went on to become alcohol abusers themselves. Whereas only 5 per cent of adoptees whose parents did not abuse alcohol went on to become alcohol abusers (Peters and Preedy, 2002).

The evidence seems to be quite clear that alcohol abuse has a hereditary basis, but how does it operate?

## Study 3.4

**AIM** Schuckit (1985) set out to investigate why the children of alcohol abusers tend to become alcohol abusers themselves.

**METHOD** A group of participants with close relatives who were alcohol abusers (high-risk group) were compared with a matched group of participants who had no close relatives who were alcohol abusers (low-risk group). Participants were given an alcoholic drink and asked to indicate how intoxicated they felt.

**RESULT** The high-risk group reported feeling less intoxicated than the low-risk group.

**CONCLUSION** The findings were used to support the view that certain people may be less able to recognise the effects of drinking alcohol. This appears to have a hereditary basis and can affect decisions about when to stop drinking. People who do not experience the symptoms of being drunk may have trouble learning when to stop.

Plomin (1990) presents a similar point of view to Schuckit (1985) when he points out that it is unlikely that we have genes that 'drive us to drink'. He suggests that the hereditary effects are more likely to be in the form of an 'absence of brakes'. In other words, the psychological and physiological factors that are present in most people, which result in them stopping drinking after a certain point, are inhibited in some people who become alcohol abusers.

## PERSONALITY

Davison and Neale (2001) argue that biological factors on their own cannot completely account for individual differences in alcohol abuse. Personality has been used as one way of explaining why some people abuse alcohol and others do not. The idea is that certain personality types are more likely to abuse alcohol than others. One line of research has been to take personality measures of children and see if there is any relationship between certain personality types and alcohol abuse in adult life. There is some evidence that children who displayed high levels of anxiety and high levels of novelty seeking (e.g. restless and fidgety) were more likely to become alcohol abusers than children who displayed low to moderate levels of these traits (Davison and Neale, 2001). Extraversion is one personality dimension that has been linked with alcohol abuse. This was confirmed in a recent study carried out by Flory *et al.* (2002). They found that alcohol abuse was indeed associated with high levels of extraversion. Another aspect of personality – conscientiousness – was also found to be associated with alcohol abuse. People who had low levels of conscientiousness were also more likely to abuse alcohol (Flory *et al.*, 2002). Low levels of conscientiousness tend to be associated with people who are disorganised, haphazard, careless and undependable (McAdams, 2000). Extraversion and conscientiousness are both dimensions of a 'normal' personality, but there is some evidence that some forms of personality disorder are associated with alcohol abuse.

**Study 3.5**

**AIM** Morgenstern *et al.* (1997) set out to investigate the relationship between personality disorders and alcohol abuse.

**METHOD** A total of 336 alcohol abusers who had entered treatment for their substance abuse took part in structured interviews to identify any personality disorder and also their levels of alcohol abuse.

**RESULT** Antisocial personality disorder (APD) was associated with more severe symptoms of alcohol abuse.

**CONCLUSION** The findings were taken to support the view that certain types of personality disorder are more likely to be associated with alcohol abuse than others.

One personality disorder in particular appears to be associated with alcohol abuse – that is, antisocial personality disorder (APD). APD is one of the most common personality disorders, with approximately 3 per cent of the population being diagnosed with it at some point in their lives. The signs and symptoms of APD include a lack of concern for rules, little regard for the rights of other people, unlawful behaviour, a lack of regard for the truth, and a tendency towards physical aggression and extreme irritability. The problem is much more prevalent in males than in females. People with APD are not just at risk of alcohol abuse but also substance abuse in general. Fabrega *et al.* (1991) found that 40 per cent of people seeking therapy for APD were also engaged in some form of substance abuse. It has been suggested that alcohol abuse in the form of binge drinking may be just one form of antisocial behaviour that is part of APD (Davison and Neale, 2001). One of the problems that can arise is that alcohol can reduce the inhibitions of people with the disorder, making it more likely that they will become violent.

## EVALUATIVE COMMENT

**It has often been assumed that there is only one form of alcoholism, but Cloninger (1987) has proposed that people who abuse alcohol can be categorised into two types. Type I alcohol abuse is less severe; it occurs in both men and women, and appears to be influenced by the environment and hereditary factors. Type II alcohol abuse, on the other hand, is more severe and is normally found in men. It appears to emerge when the men are quite young and is linked with antisocial behaviour. Cloninger (1987) suggests that type II alcohol abuse may have a larger hereditary component than type I. Zucker *et al.* (1996) argue that antisocial personality disorder (APD) is responsible for the difference between the two types of alcohol abuse. Type I alcohol abusers tend not to have APD, whereas type II alcohol abusers tend to have APD. Davison and Neale (2001) propose that the two types of alcohol abusers may do so for different reasons: type I may abuse alcohol to reduce tension, whereas type II may abuse alcohol to increase pleasure.**

## Social influence and social norms

There is no doubting the enormous impact that social influence can have on a person's behaviour. Social influence in relation to substance abuse can come through a variety of sources, including the media, peer pressure and the behaviour of role models. Social influence and social norms appear to be particularly important factors in whether or not a person starts to use a particular substance. Sarafino (1990) argues that the behaviours and attitudes of role models, including parents and other important adults such as celebrities, are among important factors in determining initial substance use. However, the effect is not the same across different types of substance abuse. Stein *et al.* (1987) found that alcohol abuse was more likely to be influenced by role models such as parents, whereas other forms of substance abuse were more likely to be influenced by the behaviour of one's peers.

The behaviour of role models is one of the factors that can influence whether or not young people engage in substance use

Substance abuse commonly takes place in a social setting, in the presence of friends and peers. This means that social pressure and the encouragement of others is likely to play a role in maintaining the substance abuse (Sarafino, 1990). Adolescents tend to spend more time with their peers and less time with their families than younger children. This means that it is likely that peers will have a considerable effect on a teenager's behaviour. According to Harris (1998), children pick up the behaviours and attitudes of their peers, and carry these learned behaviours into adulthood. Support for this view comes from Killen *et al.* (1997) who point out that people who have friends who smoke are more likely to smoke than people who do not have friends who smoke.

## Study 3.6

**AIM** Garnier and Stein (2002) set out to investigate the role of peer experiences in predicting adolescent substance abuse.

**METHOD** A total of 198 families took part in a longitudinal study. Data was collected from mothers during pregnancy and from the children (when they were teenagers) approximately 18 years later. Participants completed questionnaires and took part in interviews that elicited information on a range of topics including peer substance abuse and participants' own substance abuse.

**RESULT** Substance abuse by peers was significantly associated with the teenagers' own substance abuse.

**CONCLUSION** Substance abuse is typically a social behaviour and teenagers in this study became involved with the same behaviours as their peers. The findings were interpreted as providing some support for the view that peer pressure may have encouraged the teenagers to engage in substance abuse. There was also some evidence that the teenagers who abused substances actively sought friends with similar interests to themselves.

The relationship between peer pressure and behaviour is an extremely complex one. It is now becoming recognised that becoming a member of a group of friends is an active choice on the part of adolescents. They seek out other adolescents that are similar in some way to themselves. This means that adolescents who are at risk of substance abuse are likely to associate with others who are also at risk. This is referred to as 'social selection' (Reed and Rountree, 1997).

Social norms are the informal rules that govern what is considered to be acceptable and expected behaviour in different social settings. Social norms exert a considerable influence on the way in which people behave. Some evidence for the importance of social norms comes from cross-cultural studies of substance abuse. For example, there are quite marked differences in the levels of alcohol abuse in different cultures. Helzer and Canino (1992) point out that in some countries, such as Taiwan, the level of alcohol abuse is relatively low, whereas in South Korea the level of alcohol abuse is nearly four times higher. These differences are accounted for in terms of the different social norms that operate in the different countries. In Taiwan it is considered to be appropriate to drink alcohol with meals and on ceremonial occasions, but getting drunk is considered to be highly inappropriate behaviour. In recent years in South Korea drinking with colleagues after work has become common, and heavy drinking is seen as acceptable behaviour (Nolen-Hoeksema, 2001).

More recently it has become clear that the influence of social norms is based more on what individuals *think* their peers are doing (the 'perceived norm') rather than on what they actually do (the 'actual norm'). This distinction between 'perceived norms' and 'actual norms' was identified by Perkins and Berkowitz (1986) and is referred to as the 'social norms' approach. What we think is acceptable behaviour is based on our perceptions of the behaviour of others in our social groups. The social norms approach points out that people are not very good at estimating the extent to which other people engage in certain behaviours. For example, college students nearly always overestimate how much and how often other students drink alcohol (Perkins *et al.*, 1999). What seems to happen is that people change their behaviour to bring it closer to what they think other people are doing. So if we believe that lots of other people are engaged in substance abuse we will be more likely to do it ourselves. Our misperceptions are also used to justify our own abuse to others, using statements like 'Well, everyone is doing it!' The social norms approach has formed the basis for a number of interventions, particularly in colleges in the United States. The main focus of the interventions is correcting the misperceptions of students about the extent to which others are engaged in substance abuse.

## EVALUATIVE COMMENT

**Peer influence appears to play an important role in determining whether or not a person engages in substance abuse. However, there are some personal factors that can make people more or less likely to be influenced by their peers. For example, individuals with high levels of self-efficacy (Bandura, 1997) appear to be less influenced by their peers when making judgements about possible substance abuse (Stacy *et al.*, 1992).**

# 3.4 Effectiveness of different treatment techniques

## Aversion strategies

Aversion therapy has a long history in the treatment of substance abuse. Frawley and Smith (1990) argue that it was first used in the treatment of alcohol abuse in 1935. Since then a number of different aversion strategies have been used in an attempt to treat people who abuse substances. The general aim of aversion therapies is to ensure that the substance abuse is not rewarded. The basic principles behind aversion conditioning come from the behaviourist ideas of classical conditioning. In aversion therapy the abused substance is paired with an unpleasant stimulus such as an electric shock or a drug that makes people sick when they use the substance. In this way the electric shock, or the experience of being sick, becomes a conditioned response to the substance. Aversion strategies have been used extensively with people who abuse alcohol. The process of conditioning in aversion therapy for alcoholics is shown in Figure 3.13 on page 72.

There is evidence that aversive conditioning is an effective way of reducing alcohol abuse, although the aversive conditioning does appear to weaken over time and sessions are usually needed to reinforce it (Schuckit, 1995). Meyer and Chesser (1970) reported that aversive therapy is effective for a significant number of people. They reported that approximately 50 per cent of

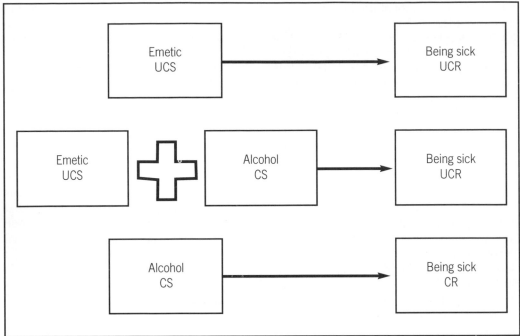

**Figure 3.13:** The process of classical conditioning in alcohol abuse aversion therapy (note: an emetic is something that makes people vomit — for example, salt water)

the people who underwent treatment did not abuse alcohol for at least a year. This is supported by Elkins (1991), who reports that with people who abuse alcohol, aversion therapy has consistently produced one-year abstinence rates in 60 per cent of patients. It also seems to be the case that aversion therapy is successful in reducing people's cravings for alcohol.

Aversive conditioning has also been used with people who want to stop smoking. As with the alcohol programmes the aim is to associate smoking with an unpleasant stimulus. A technique called 'rapid smoking' has been used where people have to inhale cigarette smoke deeply every few seconds until they start to feel ill. The idea is that the person will eventually associate the sensation of feeling ill with smoking and consequently stop smoking (Banyard, 1996)

Aversion therapy has been used most widely with people who abuse alcohol and nicotine. But there is some evidence that the techniques can be effective in the treatment of other forms of substance abuse. Bordnick (1996), and Frawley and Smith (1990) present evidence which suggests that aversion therapy can be successful in reducing the levels of craving for cocaine amongst people who abuse it. It would also seem to be the case that aversion therapy can be used successfully with heroin abusers (Lubetkin and Fishman, 1974; Thomason and Rathod, 1968). However, approaches to treating substance abuse these days rarely rely on one single form of treatment. Patients are normally treated using a multi-modal approach in which a combination of methods will be used.

Covert sensitisation therapy is an alternative form of aversion therapy. The aim here is to try and associate highly unpleasant thoughts with substance use. For example, in dealing with someone who is an alcohol abuser, the therapist might describe an imaginary scenario in which the client takes a drink of alcohol and starts feeling a burning sensation in their throat. This is followed by a description, in graphic detail, of the client being sick. It would seem to be the case that covert sensitisation techniques are an effective form of conditioning and reduce levels of alcohol intake (Nolen-Hoeksema, 2001).

## EVALUATIVE COMMENT

**One of the problems faced by some people who abuse alcohol is that they become classically conditioned to aspects of their environment. For example, many people report a desire to drink when they see their favourite drink. This appears to be the result of a conditioned response and can be the cause of relapse (Nolen-Hoeksema, 2001). Rankin *et al.* (1983) have developed a technique called cue exposure and response prevention, which aims to extinguish conditioned responses to aspects of a person's environment. Alcohol abusers are encouraged to hold a glass of their favourite alcohol close to their mouths but are not allowed to drink any. This appears to have reduced people's desire to drink and also makes it more likely that they will avoid drinking when they have the opportunity to do so.**

## Self-management strategies

Self-management strategies to substance abuse use a variety of techniques to support people who are attempting to stop their substance abuse. Self-management of substance abuse is usually carried out under the supervision of a health-care professional. Ogden (2000) suggests that during the process of self-management of their substance abuse, individuals will often be asked to engage in activities that enable them to:

- monitor their substance abuse – this could involve keeping a record of how often they abuse substances and where the abuse takes place

- develop an awareness of the reasons why they engage in substance abuse and also develop a better understanding of the causes of substance abuse

- increase their awareness of the consequences of substance abuse, and also develop a better understanding of the impact that the substance abuse has on their lives.

Self-management strategies have been used in the treatment of several different forms of substance abuse. Budney and Higgins (1998) describe a method for the treatment of cocaine abuse involving a significant self-management component. The self-management is based on an analysis of the factors that are likely to result in the persons taking cocaine. These factors are often referred to as 'triggers', and normally include the presence of certain individuals, particular places and certain feelings. Once the triggers have been identified, the aim of self-management therapy is to develop ways of coping with them in such a way that substance abuse is avoided. Typically the strategies will be jointly developed between the therapist and the client. There is some evidence that self-management strategies can be effective. Griffin *et al.* (2001) have reported that adolescents who use behavioural self-management strategies have been shown to report reduced rates of early-stage substance use.

## EVALUATIVE COMMENT

**On their own, self-management strategies appear to be no more successful than other treatment approaches (Ogden, 2000). It has been argued that as many as one-third of substance abusers relapse as a direct result of pressure from friends (Budney and Higgins, 1998). One of the problems facing the majority of substance abusers is that when they are trying to stop they come into contact with friends and acquaintances who are still using. Therefore developing the skills to refuse to abuse a substance when under direct pressure from other users is very important. This is referred to as 'refusal training' and typically forms part of a self-management programme. One of the first stages of refusal training involves helping people develop their own style of saying 'no'. This is normally followed by a number of role-playing sessions that provide the opportunity for people to practise their skills.**

## 3.5 Prevention techniques

Prevention techniques have frequently been classified into primary prevention, secondary prevention and tertiary prevention (Figure 3.14).

Although it is possible to identify different types of prevention activity, in practice it is common for interventions to use more than one level.

| Type of prevention activity | Description |
| --- | --- |
| Primary | Concerned with preventing the onset of substance abuse; typically aimed at children and young people |
| Secondary | Concerned with preventing people at risk from developing substance abuse |
| Tertiary | Concerned with preventing people engaged in substance abuse from developing further problems |

Figure 3.14: Classification of different prevention activities (from Drummond, 2002)

## REFLECTIVE Activity

Imagine you are responsible for designing an intervention aimed at preventing teenagers abusing solvents.

What factors would you consider when you designed the prevention activities?

Which levels of prevention activity would you use?

What would the prevention activities consist of?

### Knowledge of 'risk' groups

One of the ways of preventing substance abuse is to identify and target groups of people that are most at risk of developing the problem. Typically, interventions have been aimed at fairly broad groups such as young people. One of the problems with this approach is defining what constitutes an 'at risk' group. Naidoo and Wills (1998) argue that risk can be defined on the basis of either psychosocial, or cultural or biological factors. Psychosocial factors include whether or not a person is in employment, their level of social support, and whether or not they have appropriate living accommodation. People who are unemployed, have low levels of social support and are homeless are at risk of becoming involved in substance abuse. Cultural factors refer to the fact that certain ethnic groups appear to be at greater risk of substance abuse than others. For example, it would appear to be the case that although fewer Aboriginal Australians drink than non-Aboriginal Australians, those Aboriginal people that do are more likely to do so excessively (Gray et al., 2000). Biological risk factors include having a parent or parents who engage in substance abuse. There is strong evidence that some forms of substance abuse have a hereditary component – for example, alcohol abuse. So cultural, psychosocial and biological factors can be used as the basis for identifying groups of people that are at risk of substance abuse.

One of the ways in which individuals who are at 'high risk' of developing a substance abuse problem can be identified is through their contact with health-care professionals. For example, many substance abusers will make regular visits to see their family doctor or general practitioner (GP). There is some evidence that early interventions by GPs are effective in reducing levels of substance abuse amongst their patients (Anderson, 1993). Hansen et al. (1999) argue that GPs are well placed to identify substance abusers, in particular those who abuse alcohol. Support for the effective role of GPs in reducing substance abuse levels comes from Wallace et al.

(1988). They found a significant reduction in alcohol consumption amongst people who received advice from their GP.

Many substance abusers find themselves in hospital accident and emergency (A&E) departments at some point in their lives as a direct consequence of their substance abuse. This provides an opportunity to target individuals who are at risk. Drummond (2002) reports a pilot study based in two A&E departments where people were identified with an alcohol abuse problem. Individuals were invited to attend a clinic where they could discuss their alcohol abuse. Approximately half of the people identified turned up the following day

Certain ethnic groups appear to be at greater risk of substance abuse than others; this information can be used in the design of substance abuse prevention programmes

to discuss their alcohol abuse with a health-care professional. One of the criticisms levelled at interventions aimed at high-risk groups is that they focus too heavily on the individual and tend to neglect sociocultural factors.

## EVALUATIVE COMMENT

**People at risk of developing a substance abuse problem typically have dealings at some point with social services, the health system or the legal system. This is one of the reasons behind a recent government initiative in the UK, which has resulted in the establishment of drug action teams (DATs) around the country. DATs contain representatives from seven different organisations that have an interest in substance abuse (social services, the police, education services and the health authority, for example, all have representatives on DATs). Setting up DATs was an attempt to combine education, prevention and treatment services with support for criminal justice initiatives. One of the aims of DATs is to identify and help people who have been identified as being at high risk of substance abuse.**

## Fear-arousing appeals

A study carried out by Janis and Feshbach (1953) highlights the problems associated with fear appeals as a preventative measure. They designed three lectures that varied in the amount of fear they were designed to cause in the audience. The lectures were on the dangers of tooth decay, and Janis and Feshbach (1953) were interested in the extent to which a 'fear-arousing' lecture would result in behaviour change. The 'strong fear' lecture created the most worry in the participants and was also rated as more interesting than the other two talks. However, it led to the least change in dental hygiene habits. The lecture that created the least worry and fear amongst the participants was also the one that resulted in the greatest levels of behaviour change.

The findings of Janis and Feshbach (1953) are particularly relevant given the fact that many substance abuse prevention programmes are designed to give fear-arousing warnings about the future health consequences of substance abuse. Flay (1985), in a review of smoking prevention studies, points out that the fear-arousing approach is not very effective at reducing the onset of smoking. The assumption that if people know why substance abuse is bad for them and are aware of the potential adverse effects of substance abuse they will not use the substance is incorrect (Sarafino, 1990). There is little evidence to suggest that fear-arousing appeals are an effective way of preventing substance abuse.

## EVALUATIVE COMMENT

**One of the problems with fear-arousing appeals is that they do not take into account the reasons why people decide to abuse substances. Fear-arousing appeals tend to be addressed at the general population, which means that both males and females receive the same messages. However, there are gender differences related to substance abuse, particularly among adolescents. This fact has been somewhat neglected in the design of substance abuse prevention programmes in general. There is evidence that some programmes are more effective for females whereas others seem to be more effective for males (Blake *et al.*, 2001). This would seem to suggest that interventions should be designed differently for different groups in the population.**

## Health promotion/education

Like many concepts in the social sciences our understanding of what is meant by 'health promotion' is continually evolving. In the 1970s health promotion was more or less defined in terms of stopping some form of behaviour that was seen as potentially harmful. For example, reducing levels of substance abuse, in particular alcohol and cigarette use, was the focus of many health-promotion initiatives. More recently, the concept of health promotion has been expanded to include health education as well. So, in other words, health promotion in its broadest sense is concerned with enabling people to increase control over their health and consequently improve it. One of the characteristics of health-promotion interventions is that they are aimed at all individuals and not only those that have been identified as having a problem (Ogden, 2000). This means that health-promotion/education interventions can be based in a variety of settings – for example, schools, workplaces, health centres, prisons and local communities. On the other hand, some health promotion interventions are aimed at the whole population. Kaplan *et al.* (1993) argue that health-education programmes are effective at producing changes in attitudes and knowledge, but rarely lead to changes in substance abuse behaviour.

In many cases psychological theory is used to inform the design of health promotion interventions. For example, the health belief model (Rosenstock, 1966) and the theory of planned action (Ajzen, 1988) have been widely used. As far as substance abuse is concerned, the model of behaviour change proposed by Prochaska *et al.* (1992) has been widely used. Their model of behaviour change proposes that there are five stages in the process of behaviour change (Figure 3.16).

The stages in the model proposed by Prochaska *et al.* (1992) are as follows.

1. *Precontemplation* – In this stage the person is not aware that they have a problem and have no intention of changing their behaviour.

2. *Contemplation* – By the time they reach this stage the person has become aware that they have a problem. They are starting to think about how they might go about changing their behaviour, but they haven't actually committed themselves to it. There is no limit on how long people can stay in this stage. For example, Prochaska *et al.* (1992) point out that some substance abusers in their own research remained in this stage for over two years.

3. *Preparation* – In this stage the person has decided that they are going to change their behaviour in the near future. They may have already made steps to reduce the level of their substance abuse.

4. *Action* – This is the stage in which people actually change their behaviour. Once a person has successfully altered their behaviour for at least one day they can be said to be in the action stage.

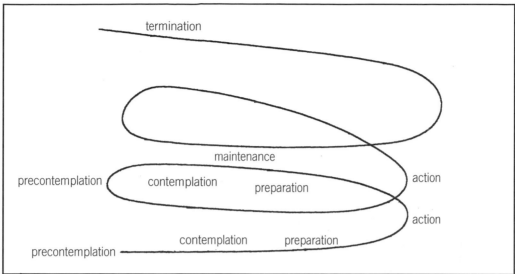

**Figure 3.16:** Simplified representation of Prochaska *et al.*'s (1992) model of behaviour change

**5.** *Maintenance* – In this stage the person has to try and avoid having a relapse. If a person has not abused a substance for at least six months they can be considered to be in the maintenance stage.

One of the key features of the model of change proposed by Prochaska *et al.* (1992) is that it recognises that most people who attempt to change their substance abuse behaviour will not be successful at the first attempt. The spiral of change in Figure 3.16 takes account of the fact that most people will have to go through the action stage at least three or four times before they successfully reach the maintenance stage.

## EVALUATIVE COMMENT

In general health-promotion/education programmes aimed at adolescents have not been very effective in terms of changing their behaviour (Banyard, 1996). However, those health-promotion interventions that are successful appear to have certain characteristics in common. For example, Flora and Thoreson (1988) have identified the following features that are common to successful anti-smoking campaigns:

- role-play scenarios to develop social skills
- information on the immediate physiological effects of substance abuse
- making a public commitment to behave in particular ways
- discussions about the influence of family and peers
- providing accurate information about the consequences of substance abuse.

## Social 'inoculation'

The social inoculation approach relies on procedures that in some way protect people from the social pressures that could result in them abusing a substance. This will typically include developing a range of personal and social skills. Although social inoculation approaches vary in their design it is possible to identify some common features. Flay *et al.* (1985) identify four components that appear to feature in the majority of social inoculation approaches (Figure 3.18). They are: first, knowledge about the consequences of substance abuse; second, an understanding of how attitudes towards substance abuse develop and are influenced by peers, family members and the media; third, development of specific skills; and, fourth, enabling individuals to make a public statement about their commitment not to engage in substance abuse.

| |
|---|
| • The health and social consequences of substance abuse are presented |
| • Discussions and information about how peers, family members and the media influence substance abuse |
| • Role-playing of specific skills such as saying 'No!' |
| • Individuals decide whether or not they will engage in substance abuse and announce this publicly to their peers |

Figure 3.18: Typical components of a social inoculation programme (based on Flay *et al.*, 1985)

## PRACTICAL Activity

Identify one substance that has been discussed in this chapter and design a social inoculation programme aimed at a secondary school.

Imagine you have implemented the programme. How would you go about evaluating whether or not it had been effective?

**Study 3.7**

**AIM** Cuijpers *et al.* (2002) set out to evaluate the effectiveness of a school-based social inoculation programme designed to prevent substance abuse. The programme is currently being used in approximately 70 per cent of schools in Holland.

**METHOD** The self-reported behaviour of a sample of pupils taken from schools that used the programme was compared with a sample of pupils taken from schools that did not use the programme.

**RESULT** It was found that pupils in the schools that used the programme reported drinking significantly less alcohol. However, cannabis use was significantly higher in schools that used the programme

**CONCLUSION** The results were taken to support the view that the programme can have an effect on the levels of substance abuse in children.

The evaluation study carried out by Cuijpers *et al.* (2002) provides some support for the effectiveness of school-based programmes. The increase in the level of cannabis use is rather problematic for the programme and needs to be considered in more detail in future research. Overall, the study demonstrates that substance use and abuse amongst children is a very complex issue. There are no simple solutions to preventing substance abuse, and the findings of Cuijpers *et al.* (2002) show us that in some cases interventions aimed at reducing substance use can actually have the opposite effect in the short term.

Social pressures are an important factor in the development of substance abuse behaviour; some prevention techniques try to provide people with skills that will help them to cope with peer pressure

## EVALUATIVE COMMENT

Another approach that is becoming increasingly popular is referred to as the 'harm reduction' approach. This approach accepts that not all substance abusers are able or willing to stop their harmful behaviour. The aim of the 'harm reduction' approach is to reduce levels of substance abuse and minimise the potential harm that people do to themselves and others. One example of this is the 'needle exchange' schemes that have been developed throughout the country. In these schemes substance abusers who use injections as a means of getting the substance into their body can exchange used syringes for new and unused syringes. One of the main dangers in sharing syringes is the possibility of becoming infected with a virus such as HIV or hepatitis C. By providing people with clean equipment it is hoped that the spread of life-threatening viruses can be reduced.

## 3.6 Sample questions

### SAMPLE QUESTION

(a)   Using an example, explain what is meant by 'physical dependence' in relation to substance abuse.
*(AO1 = 2, AO2 = 2)*                                                                     *(4 marks)*

(b)   Explain two possible effects that solvent abuse may have on the abuser.
*(AO1 = 2, AO2 = 2)*                                                                     *(4 marks)*

(c)   Describe and discuss the role of hereditary factors in alcohol abuse. Refer to evidence in your answer.
*(AO1 = 6, AO2 = 6)*                                                                    *(12 marks)*

Total AO1 marks = 10  Total AO2 marks = 10  Total = 20 marks

### QUESTIONS, ANSWERS AND COMMENTS

(a)   Outline and briefly discuss the use of aversion therapy in the treatment of alcohol abuse.
*(AO1 = 2, AO2 = 2)*                                                                     *(4 marks)*

(b)   Explain what is meant by 'tolerance' and 'withdrawal' in relation to substance abuse.
*(AO1 = 2, AO2 = 2)*                                                                     *(4 marks)*

(c   Describe and discuss the role of personality factors in alcohol abuse. Refer to evidence in your answer.
*(AO1 = 6, AO2 = 6)*                                                                    *(12 marks)*

Total AO1 marks = 10  Total AO2 marks = 10  Total = 20 marks

## Answer to (a)

Aversion therapy has been used quite a lot in the treatment of alcohol abuse. Aversion therapy is based on classical conditioning. The main aim of aversion therapy is to pair drinking alcohol with an unpleasant stimulus. The process of conditioning is shown in the diagram below.

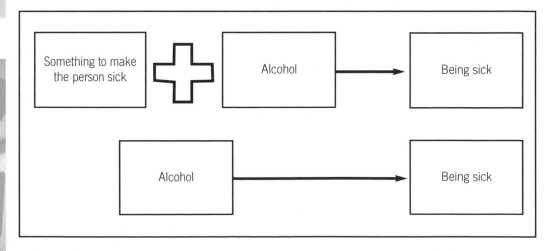

The patient will be given something to make them sick and then be given some alcohol to drink. They will drink the alcohol and then be sick. In this way, and after several trials, the person will associate the unpleasant feeling of being sick with drinking alcohol. Eventually the alcohol will become the conditioned stimulus and the person will feel sick when they look at it. There is evidence that aversion therapy is successful in stopping some people from abusing alcohol. Elkins (1991) reported that approximately 60 per cent of people who undergo aversion therapy stop drinking for at least a year. One form of aversion therapy is referred to as covert sensitisation. In this form of therapy, the UCS is in fact an unpleasant thought or image. The alcohol is associated with this unpleasant image through a process of classical conditioning.

**Comment:** This answer would be awarded the full 4 marks. The candidate provides an accurate description of aversion therapy and also points out how effective it is. The answer also briefly describes an alternative form of aversion therapy. The use of the diagram is very helpful because it demonstrates that the candidate clearly understands the process of classical conditioning that forms the basis of aversion therapy.

# Answer to (b)

When a person abuses a substance over a period of time their body starts to adapt to it. One of the side effects is that the person needs more of the substance to get the same effect. This means that they are developing a tolerance to the substance. For example, the first time you drink alcohol you only need a small amount to feel the effect. But when you have been drinking alcohol for some time you need more and more to get the same effect. At some point these effects level off.

Withdrawal means taking the drugs away from a substance abuser.

**Comment:** This answer would be awarded 2 marks. The candidate clearly understands the concept of tolerance but there will be no marks awarded for the concept of withdrawal. Withdrawal refers to the symptoms experienced by a person who has become dependent on a substance.

# Answer to (c)

Research into the relationship between alcohol and personality has looked at 'normal' personality and also people with a personality disorder. There is some evidence that alcohol abuse has a hereditary component. Some research has measured the personality of children and then looked to see if there is any link between childhood personality and alcohol abuse as an adult. There does seem to be some evidence that certain childhood personality characteristics are associated with alcohol abuse in later life. Children who have high levels of anxiety and high levels of novelty-seeking (in other words, they are restless and fidgety) appear to have a tendency to abuse alcohol later in life. Flory *et al.* (2002) found that two personality traits are associated with alcohol abuse. People with high levels of extraversion are more likely to abuse alcohol than introverts. Flory *et al.* (2002) also found that people with low levels of conscientiousness are more likely to abuse alcohol than people with high levels. People with low levels of conscientiousness tend to be disorganised and haphazard. They also tend to be undependable. So there does seem to be a link between childhood personality traits and alcohol abuse, and also in adult life certain personality traits appear to be associated with alcohol abuse. There is also some evidence that people with a personality disorder might also be at risk from alcohol abuse. Morgenstern *et al.* (1997) interviewed a number of people who had entered treatment for alcohol abuse. They found that people with antisocial personality disorder were also likely to experience severe symptoms of alcohol abuse. Antisocial personality disorder is one of the most common forms of personality disorder and approximately 3 per cent of the population suffer from it. People with antisocial personality disorder tend to have little regard for rules, be irritable and aggressive. It has been suggested by Cloninger (1987) that there are two types of alcohol abuse, one type that is associated with antisocial personality disorder and the other that is not.

**Comment:** This is a good answer and would be awarded 10 out of the 12 marks. However, the answer does not really make any reference to other factors, such as heredity, which are

associated with alcohol abuse. Although the candidate does say that heredity has a role to play they do not go on to talk about it in more detail. When answering a question like this it is important to demonstrate an understanding of the fact that there is no single factor responsible for alcohol abuse. Personality, heredity and environmental factors all play a role in determining whether or not a person abuses alcohol. The answer does present evidence to support the points made and is accurate throughout.

# 3.7 FURTHER READING

## Introductory texts

Banyard, P. 1996: **Applying Psychology to Health**. Hodder & Stoughton, London

Drugscope 2001: **Drug Abuse Briefing – A Guide to the Non-Medical use of Drugs in Britain**, Drugscope, London

Ogden, J. 2000: **Health Psychology: A Textbook**. Open University Press, Buckingham

## Specialist sources

Caan, W. & de Belleroche, J. (eds) 2002: **Drink, Drugs and Dependence: From Science to Clinical Practice**. Routledge, London

Nolen-Hoeksema, S. 2001: **Abnormal Psychology**. McGraw-Hill, New York

Sarafino, E.P. 2001: **Health Psychology: Biopsychosocial Interactions**. John Wiley & Sons, Chichester

# 4

# Criminological psychology

## 4.1 Introduction

Many of the principles and theories within psychology are able to help our understanding of crime and criminal behaviour. Consider the following example. Harry has spent much of his adult life in prison. An intelligent and outgoing individual he was doted upon by his parents as a child, but was frequently in trouble with the police, and matters came to a head when he killed someone during a robbery. In Harry's case, just as with many criminals, it is difficult to pinpoint precise reasons for his criminal conduct; we could attribute the responsibility to his parents, or perhaps he befriended others with criminal intentions. Generally speaking, most people will have a view as to why there may be so much crime around, why people commit crimes and what should be done to punish offenders in our society. Criminological psychology tries to answer questions such as these, but before considering some of the theories that psychologists apply to criminal behaviour, we need to consider what is meant by crime.

Initially, this may seem quite straightforward but even deciding if a crime has been committed can present problems. For instance, if a man plots to kill his boss but does nothing about it has a crime been committed? Alternatively, if someone witnesses a person drowning in a river but does not attempt to save them, are they guilty of a criminal offence? Finally, a young woman is attacked and in defending herself inflicts serious injuries upon the other person. Has she committed a crime?

## 4.2 The nature and measurement of offending

Every time we pick up a newspaper, listen to a news broadcast on the radio or watch a news report on television, it is likely that some mention will be made of crime. Indeed, fictional programmes and documentaries on television regularly sustain our fascination with this subject, and politicians frequently debate the crime figures, as well as what to do with the seemingly ever-increasing prison population.

## PRACTICAL Activity

Read the following list:

- driving a car whilst under the influence of alcohol
- shoplifting
- arson.

These are all clearly criminal acts but some might be seen as more serious than others.

Now write a list of other activities that are considered to be crimes (adding them to the ones above) and place these in order according to which you believe are the most serious to the least serious. What determines the 'seriousness' of a crime?

Obtain a selection of newspapers and find information on different types of crime. Consider what these different activities have in common with each other, and then use this information to arrive at your own definition of crime.

## Defining crime

Upon completing the above activity you will be aware that crime can occur on many levels, ranging from the petty theft of small amounts of money or goods to the injury or death of another person. In attempting to define crime you may notice that all of the offences are closely linked with acts that are regarded as being against the criminal law – that is, they are viewed from a legal perspective. Some definitions of crime are given below:

- 'a wrong to society involving the breach of a legal rule' (Williams, 1991)
- 'something which is against the criminal law' (Croall, 1998)
- 'behaviour that breaks the formal written laws of a given society' (Kirby *et al.*, 2000).

## REFLECTIVE Activity

Consider the definitions of crime given above and, using appropriate resources, find alternative ones.

Write down the advantages and disadvantages of these definitions. Are there some behaviours society considers 'wrong' that are not crimes in the legal sense of the word?

In summary, there are a number of related issues concerning the ways in which crime is defined. Crime is also linked to deviance (are all deviant acts criminal acts?), and it has to be considered not only from a legal viewpoint, but from social and political ones too.

### EVALUATIVE COMMENT

**When is a crime not a crime? Several problems arise when trying to define acts as crimes. Historically, for instance, witchcraft was regarded as criminal behaviour punishable by death; now, hundreds of years later, it is barely even thought of by the majority of people. Crimes also vary depending upon cultural factors, as in many countries strict religious laws govern the behaviour of the population, and offenders (such as those committing adultery) are often very harshly dealt with. Political issues can also play a major role as governments sometimes 'criminalise' or 'decriminalise' behaviours by either adding them to or removing them from the list of illegal acts. For example, in an effort to control the rave scene in Britain in the 1980s, laws were introduced to prevent large groups of people from gathering in certain places. More recently cannabis has been reclassified and is no longer labelled as a Class A drug, with first offenders now more likely to be cautioned than arrested.**

## Criminal statistics and the measurement of crime

Considering some of the problems in trying to arrive at a definition of crime, further difficulties ensue when attempting to measure the amount of crime that occurs. Newspaper headlines frequently report that the 'crime rate is soaring' or that 'crime is on the decrease', but what are such statements based upon, and are they reliable?

The police play an important role not only in detecting crime but also in recording it

### OFFICIAL STATISTICS

'Official statistics' comprise those collected by various government agencies such as the police, courts and prison service. The Home Office annually produces a document entitled *Criminal Statistics England and Wales* (with similar reports being produced for Scotland and Northern Ireland). This document collates all of the reported and recorded crime over a given period and as such represents the 'official' figures concerning what is known about the extent of crime in the country. A useful source of information on this and related issues is the Home Office website (www.homeoffice.gov.uk). The information that *Criminal Statistics* provides has a number of uses, and it can, for example, provide the police with information that will allow them to direct their resources toward certain types of criminal activity. Measuring crime, however, is extremely problematic; several agencies (such as HM Customs & Excise) maintain their own records, and even police recording practices have been shown to be potentially misleading, as the study below illustrates.

## Study 4.1

**AIM** Farrington and Dowds (1984) were interested in why there appeared to be more crimes occurring in Nottinghamshire (as measured by the official statistics for 1981) compared with quite similar counties such as Staffordshire and Leicestershire.

**METHOD** They gathered a random sample of the crime reports for each of these comparable counties, and in particular examined the police recording practices in use at the time by each force. It was speculated that several reasons could account for the disparity in figures, including the possibility that Nottinghamshire was a county in which crime was more prevalent.

**RESULT** On examination of the recording practices, it was noted that two factors emerged: first, individuals detained for one particular offence also admitted others of which the police were unaware; second, the Nottinghamshire police were more likely to record property offences of £10 or less (which the other counties may have discarded as being too trivial to pursue).

**CONCLUSION** A major reason for the marked increase in the crime figures for the county of Nottinghamshire was the way in which this particular police force chose to record the amount of crime occurring. Crime rates may thus be influenced by the perception of seriousness that each (illegal) act is given.

Criminologists have long since queried the extent to which the 'official picture' represents the true scale of criminal activity, and many regard the published figures to be only the tip of the iceberg. Beneath the surface, it is suggested, lies a vast amount of crime that does not appear in the statistics. This refers to crimes that are not reported, or not recorded by the police and other agencies, and is known as the 'dark figure' (see Figure 4.2).

## PRACTICAL Activity

It has been suggested that many forms of criminal activity are simply not reported to the police, and a direct consequence of this is that crimes known to the police may represent only a fraction of those actually occurring.

Make a list of the reasons why crimes may not be reported to the police, and give reasons why the police may not record crimes that have been reported to them.

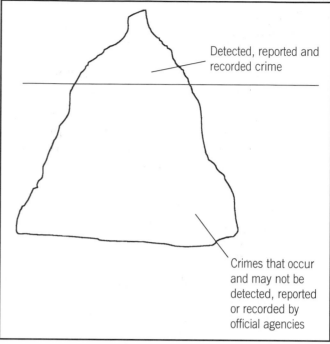

Detected, reported and recorded crime

Crimes that occur and may not be detected, reported or recorded by official agencies

Figure 4.2: The 'dark figure' of crime

If, then, the official statistics represent only a small portion of the 'true' extent of crime how can the 'dark figure' be assessed? Two main methods have been employed: self-report studies and victimisation (victim) studies.

Self-report studies involve asking individuals (in confidence) either by questionnaire or interview to indicate crimes they have committed. Such studies have been popular for several decades in the United States, and the logic behind them seems clear: a useful way to uncover criminal acts that have occurred is to ask the individuals responsible. However, a number of problems have become apparent. Many studies used young people in their samples and so it is likely that the individuals concerned may have exaggerated their replies. In addition, many of the items in the questionnaires cited largely juvenile acts and thus shed little light on the extent of adult crime (see Box, 1983).

Victimisation studies (or crime surveys) focus on the victim of a crime, and have been conducted in Britain since the early 1980s (see Study 4.2 on page 88). They are conducted annually on a sample of several thousand individuals aged 16 or over each of whom is asked if they (or anyone in their household) have been a victim of crime in the last year. If the individual has been 'personally' involved, then further details are extracted and the process results in data being compiled on particular categories of crime. As with self-report studies, victimisation studies reveal considerable gaps between the official statistics and those generated by alternative methods. Again, though, victimisation studies such as the British Crime Survey (BCS) have been subjected to criticism. Moore (1996), for example, highlights the fact that such studies under-represent the full extent of crime, since some types of crime (such as corporate crime) are excluded from them. More recently, local crime surveys have been conducted that supplement the figures provided by national surveys such as the BCS. One example is the Manchester Survey of Female Victims carried out in 1986.

**AIM** Kershaw, Chivite-Matthews, Thomas and Aust (2001) conducted the British Crime Survey to investigate the nature of crime and crime-related issues for that year, and in particular to give an alternative measure of the prevalence of crime to that found by the police.

**METHOD** Approximately 23 000 people aged 16 years or over from private households were interviewed and asked about their experience of being a victim of crime in the previous year.

**RESULT** The survey showed a decrease in many crimes, such as violent crime, household theft and burglary, and this was lower than the figures recorded by the police. Crime-related issues, such as fear of crime, revealed slight decreases from previous years, with most females fearing rape or attack, while males were concerned about vehicle theft.

**CONCLUSION** The lower figures for crimes recorded by the survey compared with those recorded by the police were attributed to the levels of crime being reported to the police having increased, and also to some extent, the recording practices used by the police.

## EVALUATIVE COMMENT

**Several problems have been identified with the various methods of attempting to uncover the dark figure, many of which can affect the reliability and validity of the results obtained. One particular issue of concern with regard to victimisation surveys involves measurement errors based upon the memory of the respondent. In some instances, the individual may experience memory decay and simply forget incidents that have happened (even quite recently). Another problem is known as telescoping, where the victim 'brings forward' an incident that actually occurred outside of the designated survey period, thus swelling the crime figures. For example, a person may report that they were burgled nine months ago when, in fact, it was 15 months ago. Alternatively, individuals may shift an incident backwards in time, so that it is not counted. Such problems, based on individuals' inability to accurately place crimes in their memory, have implications for the effectiveness of such surveys.**

## PRACTICAL Activity

Compile a self-report questionnaire that would be suitable for an adult sample. You will need to consider aspects such as how representative your questions or statements are for their purpose.

In your class at school or college, conduct a victim survey on theft and discuss the findings.

For both of these activities make a list of the ethical issues involved.

## Offender profiling

This technique is occasionally highlighted in cases where the police may enlist the services of a forensic psychologist to assist in tracking down a criminal, and as such it represents a direct means of applying psychological principles to the area of crime. The potential value of offender profiling may be appreciated if one considers that once a crime has been committed the police may have hundreds of suspects. Knowing, for instance, that the perpetrator may be a young, white male is unlikely to result in a swift arrest. However, a suggestion that the individual may have a criminal record, be a loner, have a loathing for those in authority and be likely to work in an unskilled job, will immediately narrow down the potential list of suspects. The Federal Bureau of Investigation (FBI) in the United States was the first to appreciate the merits of a method that enabled the exhaustive interviewing and screening of suspects to be significantly reduced, and the techniques involved have been applied with some success over the past 30 or so years.

Ainsworth (2001) refers to offender profiling as 'the process of using all the available information about a crime, a crime scene, and a victim, in order to compose a profile of the (as yet) unknown perpetrator'.

When used in conjunction with psychological theories and research, a profile can gradually be assembled that allows the police to narrow their search, and in many cases, eliminate certain individuals from their enquiries. For example, in cases of serial murder, a psychologist may make inferences about the offender's personality, their habits or prominent features of their behaviour based on information derived from the ways in which the murders were committed.

## PRACTICAL Activity

Offender profiling has been most commonly linked with very serious crimes like serial murder

Offender profiling has been used most widely with crimes such as serial murder and rape, although some efforts have been made to use its techniques for other crimes such as burglary.

Compile a checklist of behaviours and characteristics that you would use in order to build a profile of a burglar. For example, is the scene of the crime mainly private houses? Is the house left in a tidy state or is every room ransacked?

Offender profiling has developed considerably since the 1970s and two distinctive schools of thought have emerged. The US approach has focused on examining evidence left at the crime scene, gathered by the forensic team, for example. Known as 'crime scene analysis', this approach has generated a method of classifying offenders like serial killers so that agencies such as the FBI and police are able to assess the likelihood of future attacks and so direct their resources towards preventing it. Attempting to establish patterns that will allow behaviour to be better understood and perhaps predicted is one of the benefits of producing categories of offender. Hazelwood (1987), for instance, has conducted research in the USA and produced two types of murderer: the organised killer and the disorganised killer. Typically, for example, the organised murderer plans his or her crimes, whereas the disorganised criminal acts randomly.

In Britain the emphasis has been on using psychological techniques to shed light on the offender. Two of the most prominent researchers in this field are David Canter and Paul Britton, although they operate from different perspectives with regard to the nature of profiling.

Canter (1989) suggests that aspects of the crime will often reflect the everyday behaviour of the perpetrator and that from studying the evidence available at the crime scene, for instance, together with any other discernible patterns in the crime(s), it is possible to make certain assumptions about the person who committed the crime. This approach is known as investigative psychology, and works on the notion that most criminals tend to operate in a consistent manner that can shed light on the sort of person they are in general. For example, the location and time of a crime may give information about the criminal's habits. Using such techniques, Canter (1994) was able to provide a profile that assisted in the arrest of John Duffy, a serial rapist and murderer, in the 1980s. Gathering information from the crime scene such as the ways in which the offences had been carried out, Canter was eventually able to draw up a profile proposing that the individual involved lived close to where the crimes were committed and possessed a knowledge of the rail system (Duffy became known as the 'Railway Rapist'), together with other features about his age and living arrangements. Duffy was arrested and is currently serving a life sentence.

## EVALUATIVE COMMENT

**While offender profiling seems to offer a valuable means of assisting the police in the capture of dangerous criminals, it must be remembered that it only works in conjunction (and cooperation) with highly skilled forensic and medical personnel, teams of police and skilled interviewers. As Turvey (1996) points out, it 'cannot compensate for a lack of investigative skill' nor can it 'guarantee the complete and positive identification of specific subjects'. Rather, profiling should be seen as merely one tool at the disposal of those who are faced with the task of identifying and capturing those responsible.**

## REFLECTIVE Activity

Compile a list of the various techniques used that may lead to the eventual arrest of a criminal, such as interviews of witnesses (and suspects), examination of information found at the scene of the crime, and offender profiling.

Discuss the strengths and weaknesses of these methods.

# 4.3 Theories of offending

Perhaps the most intriguing question regarding the study of criminal behaviour concerns why people commit crimes. It may be, for instance, that a person commits murder because they have a brain disorder that causes them to have violent mood swings, or an individual sees a robbery portrayed in a television programme and then tries to copy it in an actual crime. Numerous theories have been proposed and for our purposes may be broadly categorised under the headings of biological, psychological and sociological. While the latter deals with the wider processes and influences from society and is extensively covered in texts elsewhere, the next section will concentrate on the first two categories.

## REFLECTIVE Activity

You will recall that five major approaches to the study of behaviour are: humanism, psychoanalysis, behaviourism, the cognitive perspective and the biological perspective.

For each of these approaches consider the key assumptions each would adopt in explaining why people commit crime. For instance, behaviourists might argue that someone is a criminal because the consequences of their behaviour are favourable – that is, they find crime rewarding. A burglar may steal for financial reward, or a teenager might vandalise property for social approval from his friends.

In addition, list the strengths and weaknesses of each approach regarding the extent to which each is able to account for criminal behaviour.

## Biological theories

Biological theories follow a deterministic perspective in that they assert that criminal behaviour has a physical origin – that is, a person is a criminal because of their genetic make-up. Perhaps the best-known account of a biological link with crime was provided by the nineteenth-century Italian doctor, Lombroso, who in 1876 argued that criminals were born rather than made. From studies of numerous members of the prison population he identified various criminal types based upon physical characteristics. These physical anomalies included the size or shape of the ears, the length of the nose and arms, the symmetry of the face and the amount of facial hair (see opposite). In his original theory, possessing five or more such qualities inevitably led to a criminal type. Criminals could thus be differentiated by the presence of certain features. For example, murderers could be distinguished by thin lips while robbers had beak-like noses. While such a theory may appear incredible, some support for Lombroso's claims was generated.

Goring (1913), for example, made a study of the physical features of thousands of English prisoners and while he could not find the distinctive peculiarities noted by Lombroso, he did determine that a common factor among the convicts was their poor level of intelligence. Since this was attributed to genetics, it seemed that Lombroso's assertions of the 'born criminal' were basically sound.

## EVALUATIVE COMMENT

**While it is possible to criticise Lombroso's theory on several counts (for example, his poor sampling procedures were often based upon mentally disturbed individuals), together with methodological flaws such as a lack of a control group, he did make a significant contribution to this field. Garland (1994) proposes that criminology as we know it today grew out of lines of inquiry such as those generated by Lombroso. Prior to his work towards the end of the nineteenth century, crime and criminal behaviour were largely the reserve of religious and philosophical debate. Lombroso was largely responsible for giving criminology a scientific credibility, in which the objective measurement and categorisation of the criminal classes could be conducted.**

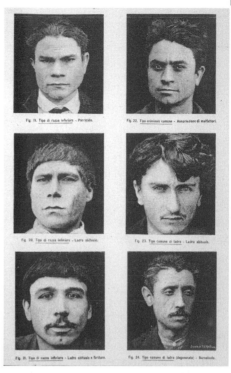

Examples of criminal 'types' from Lombroso's theory of criminality

Another contributor to this arena was Sheldon (1942), who argued that an individual's body shape was correlated with their personality. From a study of several hundred male physiques he derived three main body types (or somatotypes, see Figure 4.5 on page 92):

**1.** the ectomorph, characterised by a thin, wiry frame

**2.** the endomorph, heavy and rounded

**3.** the mesomorph, with a solid, muscular frame.

These physiques made up the three main types while the extent of each was based on a seven-point scale, with most individuals thus being a mixture of each type. More importantly, though, each somatotype was associated with a particular personality, so that the ectomorph was found to be introverted, the endomorph sociable, and the mesomorph aggressive and adventurous. With respect to criminality, Sheldon noted that from a sample of males in a rehabilitation centre, a significant proportion were mesomorphs, a finding that received support from researchers looking at other offender populations (e.g. Glueck and Glueck, 1950). One explanation of this is that the solid muscular person becomes involved in crime at an early age due to their intimidating appearance, although conceivably the individual's body shape may stem from the prison's work regime, such as doing hard manual labour.

## EVALUATIVE COMMENT

**The two biological approaches considered may seem implausible, but people often stereotype others on characteristics such as their appearance, and it is likely that certain individuals**

Figure 4.5: The
three somatotypes
(after Sheldon,
1942)

Mesomorph

Ectomorph

Endomorph

**(including the police) make 'snapshot' judgements about people that may have implications for criminal behaviour. Feldman (1977) describes a 'selection effect' that results in certain people (possibly as a result of their build) being more likely to be selected from the criminal population. It could be, for example, that the large, muscular individual is recruited by manipulative people to indulge in criminal acts. Further speculation could be that upon arriving at a crime scene, certain people are labelled by the police as having been involved in the incident.**

## PRACTICAL Activity

Using a variety of resources, collect photographs of convicted criminals. Head and shoulder pictures are more suitable for this exercise and it is preferable to use people who are not well known to the public with regard to the crime they have committed.

Cut out the photographs, place them on cards and number each one (12 should be about right). Below each picture, list five crimes (identified by a letter), one of which should be the actual crime the person committed together with four 'distracters'.

With these materials conduct a survey on an appropriate number and sample of people, in which participants are asked to identify the crime that they believe corresponds to the person pictured. Remember to be aware of ethical procedures and include a suitable debriefing. Tabulate the results and carry out an appropriate analysis to test whether people are able to correctly identify the crime that 'matches' the criminal.

Several other approaches to criminality from a biological perspective have been proposed of which the reader should be aware. These include the work on the chromosome abnormality, XYY, and also studies of twins and adopted individuals (see Study 4.3). For example, in the 1960s a line of research pursued the possibility of a criminal gene and suggested that males with this extra 'Y' chromosome were typically aggressive and violent individuals, and that this factor was possibly what led them to be criminals. However, this theory was severely criticised due to problems with the identification of the abnormal gene and also the fact that minimal differences were found between other violent offenders in prison who lacked the XYY anomaly (see Hollin, 1989). As with other topics in the nature–nurture debate, most researchers now prefer an interactionist account of behaviour.

**Study 4.3**

**AIM** Lange (1931) was interested in the extent to which identical twins might differ from non-identical twins with regard to criminal behaviour.

**METHOD** 13 pairs of monozygotic (MZ) twins were studied with regard to a variety of criminal indicators, such as possessing a criminal record, and compared with 17 pairs of dizygotic (DZ) twins.

**RESULT** Analysis of concordance rates (the extent to which twins display the same behaviour – in this case, criminal behaviour) revealed that the figure for MZ twins was much higher (77 per cent concordance) compared with that for DZ twins (12 per cent). That is, in the identical twins, over three-quarters of the sample both showed criminal behaviour, compared with just over one-tenth of the non-identical sample.

**CONCLUSION** The higher the degree of relatedness, the more likely one twin is to display the same behaviour as the other. Criminality, it seems, is in the genes.

## EVALUATIVE COMMENT

**The work on biological explanations raises a number of issues, such as the free will versus determinism debate. It will be apparent that biological views of crime are deterministic in their perspective, since they tend to argue that the individual does not act out of free will. There are however tremendous ethical implications if this argument is pursued further, since if it were possible to identify a gene for, say, psychopathy, then what should become of people who were found to carry this gene at birth? Current attempts to map out the entire human genetic make-up ('the genome project') also have tremendous implications for this area.**

**There are also a number of specific problems regarding research in this field. Twin studies, for example, have often used very small samples, which causes problems when attempting to generalise findings, and unless the twins have been reared apart it is very difficult to separate genetic effects from those of the environment.**

## Psychoanalytic theories

Psychological theories of offending have also been proposed based upon the major perspectives with which the reader should be familiar. Some of these will now be examined.

Psychoanalytical approaches to behaviour emphasise the role of early experience in determining adult personality. You should be familiar with the pioneering work of Sigmund Freud, whose theory paved the way for a new direction in the treatment of mental and behavioural disorders (see Pennington *et al.*, 2002; 2003). While Freud himself did not explore the criminal mind, other researchers have attempted to use his model as an explanation. Healy and Bronner (1936), for example, argued that criminal behaviour was a product of sublimation, a Freudian defence mechanism in which primitive impulses are redirected into other activities. According to Freud's theory, defence mechanisms serve to protect the ego (i.e. the self) when events arise that could be potentially threatening or damaging to the individual. Another example is repression, which occurs when individuals block unpleasant memories from their conscious mind. In Healy and Bronner's study, it was suggested that as a result of difficulties in establishing or maintaining emotional ties with parents, people channel this underlying dissatisfaction or unhappiness into antisocial activities. Healy and Bronner claimed support for this view in a study of children attending a behaviour guidance clinic. A group of delinquent children with a history of offences were found to have experienced more difficulties with parents, and in addition demonstrated greater emotional problems when compared with a non-delinquent group.

**Study 4.4**

**AIM** Bowlby (1944) conducted a study to investigate the link between maternal deprivation and later antisocial behaviour, and to test his maternal deprivation hypothesis in which he proposed that separation of a child from its mother in the early formative years could have psychologically harmful consequences for later development.

**METHOD** He studied two groups of boys attending a clinic for individuals with behavioural problems and compared a group of 44 juvenile thieves at the clinic with an equivalent group that did not show delinquent behaviour. The two groups were interviewed about their early experiences (especially with their mother).

**RESULT** The group of juvenile thieves was found to have experienced much more maternal deprivation than the control group. For example, approximately 39 per cent of the delinquent group had experienced up to six months of maternal separation in their first five years, while the figure was only 5 per cent for the matched group.

**CONCLUSION** Bowlby argued that maternal separation can have quite detrimental effects upon psychological health and, in particular, was a potential *cause* of delinquent behaviour.

## PRACTICAL Activity

Collect some crime reports from newspapers and magazines and analyse the content. In particular look for any references to the childhood of the offender(s) in order to identify any possible references to traumatic or emotionally painful events such as periods of separation from parent(s). Also consider other explanations for the criminal behaviour described.

## EVALUATIVE COMMENT

The notion that early experiences can have dramatic effects upon one's adult personality is intuitively appealing, and psychoanalysts such as Freud and Bowlby have enabled the implications of this process to be considered seriously. However, researchers have examined their ideas in more detail and identified several criticisms. Both theorists could be accused of adopting a confirmation bias, for instance, where only supportive evidence is highlighted and contradictory findings ignored. Bowlby's study of thieves contains a number of methodological flaws (i.e. problems in the way that the research was designed and conducted), such as a lack of control group; in addition, his findings were based on retrospective anecdotal evidence (the boys had to recall events from their own early childhood and distortions in memory are very likely). Freud's theory has been questioned from numerous angles, one major concern, for example, being that his theory does not stand up to the rigours of a true scientific approach, since it is difficult to properly test many of his central concepts. Despite this, Freud's contribution to the twentieth century (and beyond) has been immense: 'It would be hard to find in the history of ideas … someone whose influence was so immediate, so broad and so deep' (Wollheim, 1991).

## Learning theories

In contrast to the psychoanalytic perspective are learning theory approaches that stem from the principles of behaviourism. For supporters of such views *all* behaviour is learned, and this of course includes criminal behaviour. An early model by Sutherland (1939), known as 'differential association', suggested that criminal behaviour is learned through associating with other people, and that this takes place largely within close personal groups. Importantly, these groups of people need not be criminals themselves – the learning may be acquired from anyone who demonstrates views that are favourable to antisocial behaviour. In effect, this model is useful in accounting for why certain people are attracted towards a life of crime while others are not. A person may turn to crime when their definitions favourable to law-breaking exceed their definitions favourable to law-abiding (Sutherland, 1947); in other words, when the rewards to be gained for being a criminal are greater than those obtained for not being a criminal.

Skinner (1953), from his experimental work with laboratory rats, proposed several forms of training, each of which has different consequences, and which in turn leads to either a strengthening or weakening of the behaviour associated with it. Most notably, positive reinforcement entails a behaviour becoming associated with a reward so that the behaviour in question is likely to be repeated in the future. Applied to criminality, for example, if a thief breaks into a car and finds a suitcase of money, then this will reinforce their actions and make them likely to repeat the behaviour in the future. With negative reinforcement, a particular behaviour leads to an escape from an unpleasant situation, so that a person may steal in order to escape from their poverty. Alternatively a drug addict may rob someone so that they

Both positive and negative behaviours may be learned from watching others

can buy drugs and thus (temporarily) remove the withdrawal symptoms they are experiencing. While both of these methods will strengthen behaviour, Skinner also examined the role of punishment, which by contrast aims to weaken behaviour. This is achieved by administering an unpleasant stimulus when an undesirable behaviour is produced. For example, a thief, once apprehended, may receive a prison sentence that is designed to deter them from repeating their antisocial behaviour in the future.

The important role of 'social' learning was encompassed in the work of Albert Bandura (1977), who stressed the part played by observation (watching or seeing behaviour), imitation (copying the behaviour seen) and vicarious conditioning (learning the consequences of a behaviour second-hand – that is, the direct consequences may happen to someone else, but the onlooker will also learn by having observed them). Thus one may envisage an individual learning about criminal activity by seeing it carried out, and then copying what they have seen. Although not essential, if this behaviour is accompanied by rewarding consequences then the association may be quite powerful.

**Study 4.5**

**AIM** Bandura, Ross and Ross (1963) wanted to investigate the potential power of modelling by exposing children to various scenarios.

**METHOD** Children watched a film showing an adult behaving aggressively towards an inflatable clown known as a Bobo doll. Importantly, the consequences of the adult's behaviour were varied under four conditions and the researchers were interested to see if the children would imitate the behaviour they had seen. After watching the film the children were placed in the same setting with the Bobo doll.

**RESULT** The highest levels of imitation occurred in the group that had seen the model's behaviour rewarded, with much lower levels of aggressive behaviour being imitated in those who had previously witnessed such behaviour being punished.

**CONCLUSION** Aggressive behaviour may be learned by processes such as observation and imitation. This in turn has implications for various antisocial behaviours that children may acquire via role models.

## PRACTICAL Activity

Write a letter to supporters of the biological view of crime outlining the main assumptions of those adopting a learning theory perspective.

Write a reply to the first letter, outlining the strengths of the biological view, and present some criticisms of the behaviourist/social learning viewpoint.

### EVALUATIVE COMMENT

While the behaviourist perspective adheres strongly to the requirements of a scientific approach in that it is objective and theoretical, it has been criticised for its overly simplistic approach to behaviour. This argument is particularly relevant to the often complex processes involved in crime, since trying to reduce all criminal behaviour to the level of stimulus and response is fraught with difficulties. Furthermore, since many crimes are committed spontaneously by offenders and are 'opportunist' in nature, then this casts doubt upon social learning and its emphasis on observation and imitation as being instrumental in criminal activity.

## The criminal personality

Another psychological approach involves the notion that criminals differ from non-criminals on the basis of their personality. One of the most widely applied theories of personality was developed by H.J. Eysenck (1970). Presented from a biological framework the theory argued that individuals inherit a type of nervous system that affects their ability to learn from (or *condition* to) the environment.

Initially Eysenck conceived of two distinct types: extraversion/introversion and neuroticism/stability. Extraverts are typically those individuals with sociable, outgoing personalities who inherit a cortically under-aroused nervous system that leads them to actively seek stimulation in order to restore the level to an optimum. Conversely, introverts lie at the opposite end of this scale, being those of a quiet, reserved make-up, who according to Eysenck are already cortically over-aroused and thus shun sensation and stimulation. Neuroticism is shown by characteristics such as anxiety and emotional instability, whereas the opposite 'type' is a calm and even-tempered person. From this model it is possible to derive the four personality types shown in Figure 4.7 with most people being found in the middle of the range, with fewer lying at the extremes.

A later addition to the model was psychoticism, which was characterised by cold, aggressive

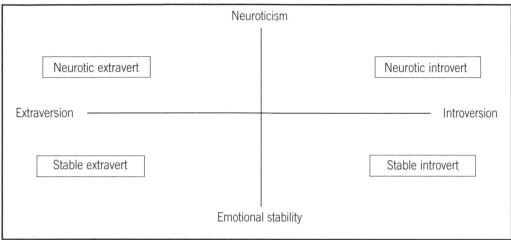

Figure 4.7: Eysenck's model of personality showing four personality types

and hostile behaviour. Based on these types, then, it is possible to speculate which combinations of features may be found among the criminal population. Each of these personality dimensions may be measured using standardised questionnaires, although as with all tests of this nature, care must be taken when interpreting the data.

## PRACTICAL Activity

Collect information concerning a variety of famous criminals from relevant sources such as newspapers, videos, books and Internet sites. In particular try to identify any information regarding their personalities.

Make a list of adjectives that can be used to describe an individual's personality, and go through the list to determine which terms may be likely to make up a 'criminal personality' (for example, cold, greedy, etc.).

Using the information you gathered earlier, apply your checklist to the famous criminals to see if there is any correspondence between their actual personalities and the characteristics you identified.

Links between this model of personality and crime become apparent when considering the level with which people adapt to their environment and in particular are able to learn society's rules. According to this theory, individuals demonstrating a high score on extraversion and neuroticism do not condition well, and so may perhaps be more common in criminal populations. Not surprisingly, the model would also predict this trend among those obtaining a high measurement on psychoticism. Indeed, research has confirmed this observation.

## REFLECTIVE Activity

In small groups discuss the strengths and weaknesses of using such scales to measure criminal personality. What effect could stereotypes and other aspects of impression formation, such as the halo effect, have on the process?

**Study 4.6**

**AIM** McGurk and McDougall (1981) were interested in the relationship between criminal behaviour and particular personality characteristics, and investigated this using Eysenck's scale.

**METHOD** Personality inventories were administered to 100 'delinquent' college students and 100 non-delinquent students.

**RESULT** Significant differences were found between the two groups of students in terms of their psychoticism (P), extraversion (E) and neuroticism (N) scores. For example, only the delinquent sample contained the combination of high scores on P, E and N, in addition to a high E and high

N cluster (which Eysenck's theory would predict). By comparison, the non-delinquent group contained a significant percentage of individuals with a low score on both E and N, again lending support to the original model.

**CONCLUSION** This study suggests that there may be a link (albeit correlational) between an individual's delinquent behaviour and their personality type.

## EVALUATIVE COMMENT

**In the above study, the sample (of 200) were all college students and so while the study is useful in highlighting differences between the personality clusters of delinquents and non-delinquents, it tells us nothing about the proportions of these groups in adult offender populations. It is thus difficult to generalise the findings of this study to these populations. Furthermore, as the findings are based upon correlations between the scores this does not allow us to assume a causal link as, often, a third unidentified factor has contributed to the outcome. In addition, personality tests themselves can bring their own problems, as often such questionnaires can suffer from respondents answering in a way that is considered 'socially desirable' rather than giving their actual beliefs or views.**

## REFLECTIVE Activity

Construct a table comparing the main theories of offending discussed above. In the table summarise the main assumptions of each approach with regard to accounting for criminal behaviour, and in addition present a brief outline of the strengths and weaknesses of each theory. Next, think of some specific crimes such as murder, burglary and fraud, and attempt to apply each theory's way of explaining these offences.

## 4.4 Treatment of the offender

So far we have considered some biological and psychological explanations for why people offend, together with ways in which crimes and criminal behaviour may be defined. If we adopt the legal perspective again, it highlights the notion of how society chooses to deal with those individuals who deliberately break the law.

### Punishment

In Britain today, a person who breaks the law may expect to receive a punishment for their crime. Depending on the seriousness of the offence this will range from a non-custodial sentence, such as a fine, through to a custodial sentence. A prison sentence remains the most severe punishment that may be imposed upon an offender in this country.

You will recall that from a behaviourist viewpoint, punishment consists of administering an unpleasant stimulus to an individual when they produce an undesirable behaviour, in order to decrease the likelihood of the behaviour being repeated. Ultimately, punishment aims to stop certain types of behaviour occurring or to prevent them from reoccurring in the future. Over the centuries, people have devised numerous methods of punishing criminals.

## PRACTICAL Activity

Make a list of the different forms of punishment (both past and present) that have been employed around the world. Consider the extent to which the punishment 'fits' the crime.

In small groups, discuss the functions of punishment. How well do you think that each of these different types of punishment results in stopping criminal behaviour?

After attempting the activity above, you may have realised that punishment can have several purposes that include not only preventing the criminal from committing further acts, but also signalling to others in society the consequences of breaking the law. Cavadino and Dignan (1997) suggest several justifications for punishment, which include:

- *deterrence* – an unpleasant experience (or the threat of one) serves to prevent the behaviour in the future

- *reform* – the experience of punishment leads the offender to becoming a 'changed' individual, such that they become rehabilitated and do not repeat the behaviour in the future

- *incapacitation* – the punishment serves to (temporarily) prevent the individual from committing further crimes by, for example, removing them from society (placing them in prison) or removing the means to re-offend (disqualification from driving)

- *retribution* – the punishment is designed to fit the crime. Here, society exacts a kind of revenge upon the offender that is considered proportional to the crime, such that a very serious crime merits a very severe punishment.

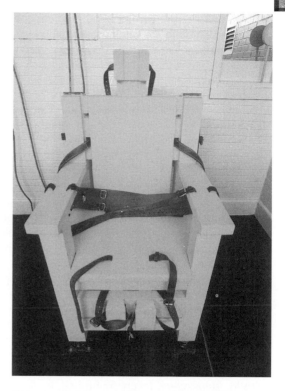

Many societies still use the death penalty to punish those who commit crimes such as murder

Essentially the first three purposes of punishment are based on the notion that punishment is justifiable since it serves to reduce the likelihood of criminal acts being repeated in the future. Deterrence does this on two levels – individual and general – so that the individual who receives the punishment is made to dwell upon their crime, and also a message goes out to the population in general, thereby deterring others (i.e. an example is made of somebody). The extent to which this is effective is, however, debatable. It has been recorded, for example, that when pickpockets were being hung in public, criminals moved through the onlookers picking their pockets!

The principle of reform is that the punishment should be based around attempting to rehabilitate the offender so that during a prison sentence, for example, the offender is treated in such a way that they undergo a 'change' in character. This latter method is far less punitive than other forms, including that of incapacitation. Here the offender is prevented from committing further offences (albeit temporarily in some cases) by some form of restriction to their behaviour being imposed. The most extreme form of incapacitation is capital punishment since the probability of the individual re-offending is zero! Other examples of incapacitation include confiscating the driving licence of a person convicted of driving under the influence of alcohol.

To some extent the electronic tagging of offenders is a form of incapacitation in that an electronic device is worn (around the ankle, for example) that sends a signal to the authorities so that the whereabouts of the offender can be monitored, and essentially restricted if required. Although such a method is much cheaper than imprisonment (which costs over £500 per inmate per week), the extent to which it ultimately 'punishes' someone is debatable.

The thinking behind retribution, on the other hand, is that offenders have transgressed the laws of society and therefore fully deserve to be punished. Taken to extremes, societies have imposed quite barbaric forms of punishment upon offenders (see Foucault, 1977); many people will be familiar with the infamous execution scene featured in the film *Braveheart*. Retribution advocates the belief in 'an eye for an eye', such that the offender receives their 'just deserts' and in this way stands in opposition to the intentions of the other forms of punishment above that all seek to reduce the future occurrence of crime. However, retribution is not always as severe as when practised in its extreme forms – the main feature is that punishment should be administered according to the seriousness of the crime and the extent to which the offender is blameworthy. For example, it would be inappropriate to send a person to prison for ten years for non-payment of a fine.

## Custodial and non-custodial sentencing

Often, depending upon the severity of the crime, the law courts have the power to impose either a custodial or a non-custodial sentence – that is, to confine the individual to a prison or other detention centre, or to confer a somewhat less severe punishment. Basically, custodial sentencing involves a prison sentence or confinement to a young offender institution (for those aged between 15 and 21).

At the present time there are over 72 000 people in prisons in England and Wales, and the arguments over whether or not this presents the best way to deal with offenders continue to gain momentum. As the prison population rises, this places considerable strain upon the resources of the service and can result in overcrowding and generally inhumane conditions as well as an increase in stress for prison staff. One possible consequence of this is rioting and disorder by the inmates, the worst case of which occurred in 1990 at Strangeways (now known as Manchester Prison), when millions of pounds' worth of damage was caused. As a result of this episode, steps were taken (published in the Woolf Report, 1991) to ensure that various recommendations were put in place, including an end to overcrowding and an improvement in sanitation to remove inhumane acts such as 'slopping out' (a procedure where inmates were required to empty their toilet waste bucket each morning after being unlocked from their cell).

There are advantages to custodial sentencing, particularly with regard to highly dangerous offenders who, for the protection of society, need to be held in secure surroundings. Several critics have argued, though, that prisons are merely 'schools of crime', and since by definition offenders are gathered together in one place, they can serve as a means of reinforcing a criminal lifestyle rather than discouraging it. It has also been claimed that prison sentences are often administered too readily and that for relatively minor crimes such as petty theft, greater use should be made of the alternatives that are available.

When a person is found to have broken the law they begin a number of steps that process them through the criminal justice system. It may be that they receive an absolute or conditional discharge, the latter requiring them to report to a police station, for example, or to restrict their movements and avoid certain people or places. Non-custodial sentences include fines, compensation orders, community service and probation. Fining an individual for an offence involves the legal system requiring the person to pay a financial penalty for their crime, although this is completely dependent on them having the means to do so. Compensation orders work on the principle of reparation – that is, having the offender 'make amends' for their crime by, for instance, recompensing the victim.

On a related note, mediation programmes are sometimes available (having been successfully pioneered in Leeds in the 1990s); these involve bringing the willing victim and offender together under supervised conditions (sometimes the offender may still be in custody). One purpose of these meetings is to allow a victim to question the offender and so perhaps try to resolve any anger they may have, such as why they were targeted for a burglary. Community service orders involve an offender being required to carry out work in the community (in a way, acting as a general form of reparation) such as clearing wasteland. In this way, it is argued, the criminal contributes something positive back to society. Finally, towards the end of the criminal justice process, is probation. A person newly released from prison may be placed under the supervision of a probation officer to whom they must report at regular intervals, and from whom they may receive help and guidance relating to their welfare. In some cases failure to report may involve a previously 'suspended' prison sentence being imposed.

# PRACTICAL Activity

Collect reports from national and local newspapers on recent crimes and, in small groups, try to decide upon the most appropriate sentence that should be given to the individual(s) concerned.

As a research exercise use the Internet and find out (a) the current population of people in prison (see www.homeoffice.gov.uk), and (b) the aim of imprisonment according to HM Prison Service.

# REFLECTIVE Activity

In small groups, write down the advantages and disadvantages of each of the various types of non-custodial sentence.

## Psychological effects of imprisonment

One of the fundamental aspects of imprisonment, regardless of the duration of the sentence imposed, is the removal of a person's liberty, which in itself will bring immediate psychological effects due to being separated from one's partner, family and friends. Longer sentences also increase the possibility of institutionalisation, where the individual becomes enveloped in the roles associated with their environment (see Goffman, 1961). This aspect is also highlighted in the study below.

**AIM** Zimbardo *et al.* (1973) conducted a study to look at the psychological effects of imprisonment by simulating a prison environment using converted rooms in the basement of Stanford University.

**METHOD** The participants in the experiment were American college students chosen from the many original applicants on the basis of their suitability for the study, and at the outset were considered to be emotionally stable, responsible and with no record of antisocial behaviour. The study was scheduled to last for two weeks and, to begin with, participants were allocated the role of prisoner or guard by tossing a coin. After being 'arrested' and escorted to the prison by police car, the behaviour of both prisoners and guards was carefully monitored.

**RESULT** Soon after the experiment commenced, an atmosphere quickly developed in which the prisoners became submissive and despondent, while the guards became arrogant and spiteful, subjecting the prisoners to demeaning rituals, and generally asserting their power over them. It soon became evident that the roles being played out were starting to have unforeseen effects, especially in the prisoners, many of whom became withdrawn and depressed, and the study was stopped after six days.

**CONCLUSION** Individuals can quickly adopt new roles and a position of authority, when abused, can have quite harmful consequences. This has implications for various professions, such as teaching or the police, where a role is invested with a degree of power over others.

Several researchers have looked at the impact of imprisonment upon the individual's mental health, with some findings indicating the existence of a form of psychosis in long-term inmates (see Blackburn, 1993). It has also been proposed that individuals become immersed in a process of socialisation known as 'prisonisation', originally defined by Clemmer (1958) as 'the taking on in greater or lesser degree of the folkways, mores, customs and general culture of the penitentiary'. This process ranges from alterations in lifestyle, such as eating and sleeping habits, to adopting

Does prison work?

prison slang and the acceptance of certain norms to reinforce the notion of 'us' and 'them' (e.g. never informing on another inmate). The consequences of such a process are dramatic as: 'the influences of these universal factors are sufficient to make a man characteristic of the penal community and probably so disrupt his personality that a happy adjustment in any community becomes next to impossible' (Clemmer, 1958).

## PRACTICAL Activity

Make a list of the various ways in which a person's behaviour may noticeably change once they enter prison. How will they be influenced by the new rules and regulations, and how may they be affected by the other prisoners, and prison staff?

Write down your impressions of what you think a prison is like and then try to organise a visit to a prison with your teacher and class. Record your observations and compare them with your original views.

### EVALUATIVE COMMENT

**One element of the prisonisation process was considered to be an outright non-conformity to the wishes of those in authority, although some research by Wheeler (1961) challenged this by finding that an inverted-U pattern existed, depending on the length of sentence. Namely, conformity to prison staff norms increased in the early and late phases of the sentence, but dipped in the middle phase.**

**Apart from the supposed linear relationship between prisonisation and sentence length, other criticisms of the concept have been put forward. For example, Blackburn (1993) argues that such a model ignores the role of individual differences – it may be that while some prisoners do find difficulty adjusting to life when released, others adapt more successfully. It must also be appreciated that the experience of imprisonment is not the same for everyone and that the type of institution, length of sentence and previous experience of prison, among other factors, may all contribute.**

## The effectiveness of custodial sentencing and the problem of recidivism

In 1993 the then Home Secretary, Michael Howard, in an address to the Conservative Party conference said, 'Let us be clear. Prison works ...'. At this point consider the official intention of imprisonment as well as some of the functions of punishment outlined above. In order to address the question of whether or not prison 'works', it is important to reflect on what purpose prison serves. Thus from the point of view of incapacitation, it does, since when an offender is in prison they cannot commit any crimes (other than offences committed whilst in jail). However, one of the major arguments against the effectiveness of custodial sentences relates to rehabilitation. Simply put, if prison develops the character of those who have experienced it so that they change their view towards crime and become law-abiding citizens upon release, then very few people should return. However, recidivism rates suggest that this is not the case. These measure the number of people that have re-offended, and statistics have shown that over 70 per cent of offenders under the age of 21 return to prison within two years of being released. There are several reasons why this figure may be especially high among young people, but it does suggest that the mere experience of being given a custodial sentence is ineffective for many people. Once released, of course, an individual will usually return to the same environment, with the same friends and associates, and coupled with factors such as a lack of money, it may be difficult to avoid committing further crimes. Critics mainly cite recidivism rates as evidence that individuals are not being reformed by their experience inside such institutions. However, a number of treatment programmes exist that, if correctly implemented, can help to lower the number of recidivists; these will be considered next.

# 4.5 Therapies used to treat offenders

Several programmes have general applications to a range of offender behaviours, and these tend to be based upon the major psychological perspectives such as humanism, psychoanalysis and behaviourism.

## Behaviour modification

The principles of operant and classical conditioning have been applied in behaviour therapy and behaviour modification techniques, where desirable behaviour is reinforced and undesirable behaviour extinguished. This has also involved the use of token-economy systems whereby positive behaviours are rewarded with tokens that may be exchanged for commodities such as cigarettes. The effectiveness of such programmes, though, has been questioned. For example, although the techniques may have short-term benefits in changing behaviour, they are less effective in the long term (see Hollin, 1989).

**Study 4.8**

**AIM** Cullen and Seddon (1981) investigated the use of token economies with people in a young offenders institution in order to see if their behaviour could be modified.

**METHOD** The boys in the programme were placed on a regime where positive behaviours such as avoiding confrontations with others were reinforced using tokens that could be exchanged at the institute's shop for items such as confectionery. Undesirable behaviours, such as hostile behaviour, were not reinforced in an effort to bring about extinction.

**RESULT** Over the duration of the study those who were placed on the token-economy system began to produce socially desirable behaviours.

**CONCLUSION** Techniques based upon the principles of learning theory can be applied successfully to modifying antisocial behaviour.

## Social skills training

Social skills training has also met with some success, and involves attempts to provide offenders with the appropriate skills and strategies that many of us take for granted, such as responding appropriately to others in social interactions. These may often include the use of role-play activities. Many offenders, particularly those in custody for violent behaviour, have been shown to lack the necessary social skills to cope with aggressive encounters, and perhaps through limited experience find great difficulty in handling day-to-day situations with other people. One feature that can be misinterpreted is non-verbal communication, and offenders can be taught various aspects such as gaze and gestures, both in 'reading' the messages that another person is

Many people lack the necessary social skills to deal with social interactions such as this

signalling and in terms of self-presentation, so that they learn what is considered an appropriate amount of eye contact to use, for example. Specific techniques such as these have been found successful. For example, Goldstein (1986) gathered the data from 30 studies of young offenders and found that they yielded positive outcomes, although this tended to be restricted to the duration of the programme. Four-fifths of those given social skills training did not generalise the techniques beyond the training environment.

## PRACTICAL Activity

Investigate the range of treatment programmes available for offenders, and design a suitable programme for the following:

1. a person who is aggressive and who reacts negatively to criticism
2. a person who is socially withdrawn and who finds it difficult to interact with others.

## REFLECTIVE Activity

Consider the strengths and weaknesses of the various programmes currently available for both long-term and short-term prisoners.

### Anger management

A somewhat more specialist intervention programme centres upon anger management and is a form of cognitive behavioural therapy. Here it is emphasised that an individual's thoughts and beliefs need to be changed in addition to modifying their behaviour. Thus a person's perceptions of a situation need to be examined, and negative beliefs changed, via therapy, to positive ones. Many offenders lack the appropriate strategies to deal with potentially aggressive situations in a non-confrontational manner, and often respond to threats or even relatively ambiguous situations with anger, which may then lead to violence (for example, a stranger accidentally bumping into them). Anger management programmes (also called anger control or anger reduction) usually involve group work in which participants learn to employ self-control and other coping skills. Three stages are normally incorporated into such programmes.

1. In *cognitive preparation*, people are encouraged to actively think about times in the past when they have become angry. This helps to identify possible triggers in the environment and also to highlight particular patterns that could be avoided in the future. In addition, the individual is encouraged to contemplate the consequences of losing their temper, and to appreciate that in the long run these can only be negative (e.g. damaging friendships).

2. *Skill acquisition* involves teaching the individual a range of cognitive and behavioural strategies so that they may deal with incidents in a more positive manner. For example, the use of positive self-talk may help to break the pattern of response that is normally used in situations that have led to outbursts of anger in the past. Behavioural techniques include the use of relaxation to counter tension.

3 *Application practice* allows the individual to put into practice the strategies and techniques they have been taught; this is often achieved by means of role-playing exercises that are conducted under supervised, controlled conditions.

**Study 4.9**

**AIM** Feindler, Marriott and Iwata (1984) conducted a study to investigate the effectiveness of anger-management techniques in reducing disorderly behaviour.

**METHOD** Children at a high school for those with behavioural and delinquency problems were placed on a programme where they were taught a variety of techniques to combat their anger. These included looking at ways to solve problems, lower tension and arousal levels, as well as strategies to develop self-control.

**RESULT** The children's behaviour was monitored (by themselves and others) and regular reports made by their teachers concerning their behaviour. Significant improvements were noted in the various criteria measured, including their degree of self-control and their problem-solving abilities. Encouragingly, these benefits were found to persist some five weeks later.

**CONCLUSION** Antisocial behaviour, such as aggression, in delinquent children can be substantially reduced using carefully controlled anger-management techniques.

## EVALUATIVE COMMENT

Undoubtedly, many of the techniques that have been used to reduce violent and aggressive behaviour have yielded some promising findings. However, Blackburn (1993) points out that many of the training programmes only appear to demonstrate short-term benefits, with offenders often returning to their previous ways soon after the study. The reasons for this decline in progress need to be examined so that improvements become part of the individual's long-term behaviour. In addition, there is a need for more studies with offenders since several of the claimed benefits are based upon research in clinical settings rather than criminal ones, so it is questionable how far the findings from one can be generalised to the other. On a similar note, studies based upon young offenders and children with behavioural and delinquency problems cannot readily be generalised to adult criminal populations.

## 4.6 Sample questions

### SAMPLE QUESTION

(a)  Distinguish between self-report studies and victimisation studies as techniques to measure crime.
     *(AO1 = 1, AO2 = 2)*                                                              *(3 marks)*

(b)  Describe *one* study in which criminal behaviour and personality was investigated.

     In your answer you should refer to why the study was conducted, the method used, the results
     obtained and the conclusions drawn.
     *(AO1 = 4, AO2 = 1)*                                                              *(5 marks)*

(c)  The Italian physician Cesare Lombroso originally argued that criminals were born rather than made.
     Discuss the extent to which criminal behaviour is a product of biological factors.
     *(AO1 = 6, AO2 = 6)*                                                             *(12 marks)*

     Total AO1 marks = 11  Total AO2 marks = 9  Total = 20 marks

### QUESTIONS, ANSWERS AND COMMENTS

(a)  Describe *two* features of Lombroso's theory of criminal behaviour.
     *(AO1 = 4)*                                                                       *(4 marks)*

(b)  Using an example, explain what is meant by non-custodial sentencing.
     *(AO1 = 2, AO2 = 2)*                                                              *(4 marks)*

(c)  Discuss *two* psychological effects that imprisonment may have upon offenders.
     *(AO1 = 4, AO2 = 8)*                                                             *(12 marks)*

     Total AO1 marks = 10  Total AO2 marks = 10  Total = 20 marks

## Answer to (a)

One feature of Lombroso's theory of criminal behaviour is the idea that criminals are born rather than
made. Another feature is that he believed that criminals could be distinguished from non-criminals by
certain distinctive physical features such as the shape of the nose.

**Comment:** A total of 3 marks are awarded for this answer; 1 mark is given for naming each
of the correctly identified features and the third for the elaboration/description of the second
feature. Full marks were not awarded because the candidate only identified the first feature
(criminal behaviour as 'born') and did not provide further details such as the belief that
criminality was due to genetics.

## Answer to (b)

Non-custodial sentencing means a sentence that is imposed on someone, which does not involve them
having to go to prison. This type of sentence is usually given because it may be the person's first
offence, or because the offence was not considered to be serious enough to deserve being sent to prison.
An example of a non-custodial sentence is a community service order.

**Comment:** Full marks are awarded for this answer. Although in places the language used is a
little basic, the main information is provided. The answer has given a 'definition' of non-
custodial sentencing (which warrants 2 marks for AO1) and in addition has elaborated upon
this with an explanation of the circumstances under which such a sentence might be
imposed (thereby gaining another mark, for AO2). The fourth mark (AO2) is given for the
example.

# Answer to (c)

One psychological effect that has been found as a result of imprisonment is that people often suffer from depression. This is often because inmates are deprived of their freedom and start to miss everything that they had out of prison. The depression may occur because they have time to dwell on their loved ones or because they have been given a long sentence and so all that they see is time stretching out in front of them for months or years. One point to make, though, is that it can depend on the individual because some people are less likely to get depressed than others. Also some studies have shown that more people tend to get depressed at the beginning of their sentence.

Another psychological effect of imprisonment is that the person may experience prisonisation. This was a term used by Clemmer in 1958 to refer to the way that a prisoner gradually learns a new set of behaviours and attitudes once they are in prison. This can include learning prison slang, as well as 'acceptable' codes of behaviour such as how to talk to prison officers. It was thought by Clemmer that this process increased the longer a person was in prison so that to keep up a tough image they did not cooperate with staff. Some work has criticised this idea, though, because Wheeler found that a U-shaped pattern existed. He said that when people first enter prison they still cooperate with staff and are not fully 'prisonised', but that towards the middle of their sentence their behaviour changes more as they become used to the 'inmate subculture'. Finally, he said that as the inmate nears the end of their sentence their behaviour becomes more cooperative again.

**Comment:** This answer shows evidence of knowledge and understanding, although it is quite descriptive and, in places, vague. However, two relevant psychological effects are referred to and these are credited. The first section on depression is less effective in its use of psychological terminology, though, and tends to be rather more anecdotal in style. The second point (prisonisation) displays a more in-depth level of knowledge and understanding, and is supported with reference to research evidence. Even here, though, there is a lack of depth or detail, and additional explanation would be helpful. For an A2 answer, though, much greater emphasis is placed upon skills of analysis and evaluation, with the marks awarded being proportioned more in this direction. In this answer there is evidence of critical consideration of the points made, but this is less thorough than would be required for a good answer. This answer was awarded 6 marks out of 12 (3 marks for AO1 and 3 marks for AO2), making a total of 13 marks for the whole question. This candidate would be advised to develop their longer, discussion-based answers by increasing their use of appropriate terminology and the range of research evidence used, so that points made can be clearly illustrated using relevant work. In particular, though, they need to work on the analytical and evaluative elements of topics so that they become better acquainted with formulating a logical, reasoned argument.

# 4.7 FURTHER READING

Introductory texts

Brewer, K. 2000: **Psychology and Crime**. Heinemann, London

Harrower, J. 1998: **Applying Psychology to Crime**. Hodder & Stoughton, London

Hollin, C.R. 1989: **Psychology and Crime: An Introduction to Criminological Psychology**. Routledge, London

Putwain, D. and Sammons, A. 2002: **Psychology and Crime**. Routledge, London

## Specialist sources

Ainsworth, P.B. 2000: **Psychology and Crime**. Longman, Harlow

Blackburn, R. 1993: **The Psychology of Criminal Conduct**. John Wiley & Sons, Chichester

Cavadino, M. & Dignan, J. 1997: **The Penal System: An Introduction**. 2nd Ed. Sage, London

Croall, H. 1998: **Crime and Society in Britain**. Longman, Harlow

Davies, M., Croall, H. & Tyrer, J. 1998: **Criminal Justice: An Introduction to the Criminal Justice System in England and Wales**. 2nd Ed. Longman, Harlow

Holdaway, S. 1988: **Crime and Deviance**. Nelson Thornes, Cheltenham

Hollin, C.R. 1992: **Criminal Behaviour: A Psychological Approach to Explanation and Prevention**. Falmer Press, London

Maguire, M., Morgan, R. & Reiner, R. (eds) 1997: **The Oxford Handbook of Criminology**. 2nd Ed. Clarendon Press, Oxford

Moore, S. 1996: **Investigating Crime and Deviance**. 2nd Ed. Collins Educational, London

Morris, N. & Rothman, D.J. (eds) 1995: **The Oxford History of the Prison**. Oxford University Press, Oxford

# Glossary

**Addiction** An addiction is a behaviour over which a person has little control, and which has harmful consequences. People that are addicted to a substance typically recognise that they are harming themselves but are unable to stop their addictive behaviour.

**Amphetamines** Stimulants that have a similar effect to cocaine.

**Antisocial personality disorder (APD)** A person with this disorder finds it difficult to form relationships and take responsibility for their actions. There is a link between antisocial personality disorder and alcohol abuse.

**Autoganzfeld studies** Studies using an automated version of the ganzfeld technique. The computer-controlled display of information prevents sensory leakage and experimenter effects.

**Aversion therapy** A therapy for substance abusers that is based on classical conditioning principles. An unpleasant stimulus, such as being sick, is paired with the substance that is being abused. This approach has had some success with people who abuse alcohol.

**Behaviour modification** Therapeutic techniques based upon the principles of operant conditioning in which undesirable behaviour is changed to desirable behaviour.

**British Crime Survey** A survey conducted on a regular basis in which large numbers of the population (in England and Wales) are questioned about the extent and nature of their having been victims of crime.

**Central nervous system** The part of the nervous system that consists of the brain and spinal cord. It supervises and coordinates the activities of the entire nervous system.

**Clairvoyance** Gathering information about objects or information that is hidden from view without using recognised sensory channels such as sight or hearing.

**Classical conditioning** A form of learning in which a neutral stimulus is paired with another stimulus (the unconditioned stimulus), which naturally gives rise to a response (the unconditioned response). After a number of trials the neutral stimulus produces the same response on its own. At this point the neutral stimulus is referred to as the conditioned stimulus and the response is called the conditioned response.

**Cocaine** A substance that relieves pain, and produces feelings of happiness and excitement in people that use it. It is classed as a stimulant and is produced from leaves of the coca plant.

**Cognitive behavioural therapy** Therapeutic techniques based on the concept of changing a person's behaviour by working on their negative thoughts and beliefs.

**Companionate love** A form of love that is characterised by a caring and trusting relationship.

**Complementarity** In interpersonal attraction, the concept that couples are drawn together based on the different qualities that each person possesses. For example, a shy person may be attracted to someone with the 'opposite' personality.

**Covert sensitisation** A form of aversion therapy in which the unpleasant stimulus is an image or a thought that is generated by the person undergoing therapy for substance abuse. The unpleasant image is paired with the substance that is being abused.

**Criminal justice system** Collective name for several agencies in society that carry out specific functions with respect to the law of the country. These include the police, courts and prisons.

**Cross-cultural study** A research method that makes comparisons across different cultural or ethnic groups.

**Custodial sentence** Sentence given out by courts to offenders, consisting of a specified length of time to be spent in a prison or other confined institution.

**Dark figure** The potentially large amount of crime that occurs that is not reported, detected or recorded by official agencies such as the police.

***Delirium tremens* (DTs)** One of the withdrawal symptoms associated with alcohol misuse. When a person stops drinking alcohol after a long period of heavy drinking they can experience hallucinations, trembling and shaking, and sweating.

**Dependence** Dependence refers to a situation where a person needs to use a substance in order to feel normal. There are two types of dependence: physical dependence and psychological dependence.

**Depressants** These substances slow down the activity of the central nervous system. Heroin is a commonly abused depressant.

**Deterministic** Term given to approaches or theories that suggest a person's behaviour is a result of some external (or internal) cause rather than having been freely chosen. Often contrasted with free will.

**Dice-throwing studies** Studies of psychokinesis in which the participant tries to influence the score when two dice are rolled. The effects can only be observed by the use of statistics.

**DMILS** 'Direct mental interaction with living systems', which refers to situations where a person can influence another living system, such as a person or animal, without using recognised sensory channels. Psychic healing is one example of DMILS.

**Dopamine** A neurotransmitter that is associated with the reward centres of the brain. Many forms of substance abuse appear to cause increased levels of dopamine in certain parts of the brain.

**Experimenter effects** When a person carrying out a study intentionally or unintentionally affects the results.

**Extra-sensory perception (ESP)** When information is acquired about a target in the environment without using recognised sensory channels. There are three recognised forms of ESP: telepathy, clairvoyance and precognition.

**File-drawer problem** A problem that arises from the fact that there is a tendency for academic journals to publish only studies with positive findings. This means that studies that do not find any significant effects tend to remain in the experimenter's filing cabinet. This has implications for meta-analyses that combine the results of several studies. If a meta-analysis is only based on studies that have significant findings then its results will be biased.

**Ganzfeld technique** A special type of environment in which a participant's sensory input is reduced. It typically includes the use of goggles and 'white noise'. It is thought that such conditions are conducive to ESP phenomena.

**Hedonistic** A view that places major importance on the obtaining of pleasure as a motivation for behaviour.

**Heroin** One of a group of drugs that are derived from the poppy plant. It can be taken in several ways, including smoking and injection.

**Hypothalamus** A structure found in the forebrain that is involved in a number of 'automatic' functions including sexual behaviour and temperature regulation.

**Korsakoff's syndrome** A chronic brain disorder marked by memory problems. Often the result of long-term alcohol abuse.

**Longitudinal study** A research method that focuses on the same group of participants over a period of time, usually in order to observe any changes in behaviour over the duration of the study.

**Macro-PK** Psychokinesis that can be observed by the naked eye – for example, moving or breaking objects.

**Maternal deprivation** Early separation of the offspring from the primary caregiver – usually, but not always, the mother – that is claimed to have harmful effects on the child's psychological development.

**Meta-analysis** A technique that enables researchers to combine the results of many studies. It is particularly useful in situations where there is a small effect size.

**Micro-PK** Psychokinesis that can only be detected using electronic or statistical methods. For example, in *dice-throwing studies*.

**Nature–nurture debate** A view held in disciplines such as psychology that behaviour is either a result of biological factors such as genetics (nature), or stems from the contribution of the environment and experience (nurture)

**Need for intimacy** A personality characteristic that reflects the extent to which a person feels the need to be emotionally close to another individual.

**Neuron** A single nerve cell found in the brain.

**Neurotransmitter** A chemical that is responsible for transmitting information from one neuron to another. For example, dopamine.

**Nicotine** The psychoactive substance in tobacco smoke. It is highly addictive.

**Offender profiling** Term used for various techniques used by criminological psychologists, whereby inferences from various sources of information (such as those found at the scene of a crime) are made, in order to build up a 'picture' of the person responsible.

**Operant conditioning** Refers to the acquisition or elimination of a behaviour as a result of the reward or punishment of a specific behaviour.

**Paranormal** The term used to describe phenomena that can not be explained by conventional science.

**Parapsychology** The term used to refer to the scientific study of paranormal phenomena such as ESP and PK.

**Passionate love** Also known as romantic love, this is a highly charged, emotional type of love, characterised by sexual arousal and intense feelings for the other person.

**Physical dependence** Develops when the body has adapted to the presence of a substance so that it needs the substance to function normally. If a person does not have a sufficient amount of the substance in their body they will experience withdrawal symptoms.

**Polysubstance abuse** The abuse of more than one substance at the same time. For example, abusing heroin and cocaine.

**Precognition** Knowledge of future events that has been obtained without using recognised sensory channels.

**psi** A term used to describe forms of communication that have occurred without using recognised sensory channels. Usually refers to both ESP and PK.

**Psychoactive substance** A substance that affects a person's mood or thought processes.

**Psychokinesis (PK)** An ability to influence a target using the mind without the aid of any physical means. Includes *macro-PK*, *micro-PK* and *DMILS* phenomena.

**Psychological dependency** Refers to a situation where a person's life has become centred around a particular substance. They rely on the substance to make them feel good.

**Random event generator (REG) studies** Research into *micro-PK*, which relies on the random generation of events involving either a computer or a radioactive source.

**Recidivism** A term used to refer to the number of people who re-offend and are reconvicted once released from prison.

**Reliability** With reference to questionnaires or tests, the extent to which the test is able to produce the same (or very similar) scores on another occasion.

**Remote viewing studies** Studies in which the participant attempts to describe scenes or objects that are some distance away and cannot be seen using conventional means.

**Replication** When other researchers repeat a study to ensure that the findings are reliable. It is important in any science to ensure that the findings of a study are not simply due to some flaw in the experimental design.

**Self-disclosure** An occurrence, usually some time into a developing relationship, where one or both of the people reveals personal information about themselves to the other.

**Self-management strategy** A technique used to support people who are attempting to stop their substance abuse. Usually the individual will monitor their abuse and develop an awareness of the causes of their substance abuse.

**Self-report study** A survey that sheds light on the amount of 'hidden crime' occurring by asking offenders to indicate criminal offences that they have committed within a certain time period. In such surveys the confidentiality of the respondent is assured (see *victimisation survey*).

**Sensory leakage** When a flaw in the experiment's design enables the participant to gain information through their normal sensory channels.

**Sexual orientation** A term used to refer to an individual's sexual preferences.

**Social cognition** A branch of psychology that is concerned with aspects of cognition such as thinking and problem-solving, and how they relate to social behaviours such as friendship and group processes. For example, children's thoughts about friendship.

**Social exchange theory** A theory of social behaviour which suggests that relationships are founded and maintained on the basis of the relative costs and benefits involved to each person.

**Social influence** The effect that the presence of others has on the way in which an individual thinks and behaves.

**Social norms** The informal rules that govern what is considered to be acceptable behaviour in different social settings.

**Solvent abuse** The abuse of solvents such as cigarette lighter fuel and glue.

**Stimulants** Substances that stimulate the central nervous system. Commonly abused stimulants include cocaine and amphetamines.

**Substance abuse** Refers to a situation where a person uses a substance to such an extent that it causes them harm.

**Substance misuse** The use of a substance in a way that results in the person experiencing social, psychological, physical or legal problems.

**Substance use** The use of a substance without any direct harm to the individual.

**Target** In a test of ESP this is the information that has to be acquired by the participant. In a test of PK it is the object or living organism that has to be influenced.

**Telepathy** The transmission of information from one person to another without using normal sensory channels such as sight and sound.

**Tolerance** When a substance is used for a period of time the body begins to adapt to it. Tolerance refers to the fact that, as some substances are used, the person starts to need more and more of them to get the same effect. The person has become tolerant to the substance.

**Triangular theory of love** Model, proposed by Sternberg (1986), that suggests love is comprised of three basic ingredients: passion, intimacy and commitment.

**Validity** With reference to questionnaires or tests, the extent to which a test is measuring what it is supposed to.

**Victimisation studies** Surveys that shed light on the amount of 'hidden crime' occurring by asking individuals if they have been the victim of particular crimes within a certain time period (see *self-report study*).

**Withdrawal effects** The symptoms that a person experience• when they suddenly stop taking a substance they have become dependent upon. Typical symptoms include cramps, sweating, restlessness and tremors.

# Bibliography

Adesso, V.J. (1985) Cognitive factors in alcohol and drug use. In M. Galizo and S.A. Maisto (eds) *Determinants of Substance Abuse: Biological, Psychological and Environmental Factors*, New York, Plenum

Ainsworth, P.B. (2001) *Psychology and Crime: Myths and Reality*, Harlow, Longman

Ajzen, I. (1988) *Attitudes, Personality and Behaviour*, Chicago, Dorsey Press

Altman, I. and Taylor, D.A. (1973) *Social Penetration: The Development of Interpersonal Relationships*, New York, Holt, Rinehart & Winston

Anderson, P. (1993) Management of alcohol problems: the role of the general practitioner, *Alcohol & Alcoholism* 28(3), 263–72

Anderson, R.H., Fleming, D.E., Rhees, R.W. and Kinghorn, E. (1986) Relationships between sexual activity, plasma testosterone and the volume of the sexually dimorphic nucleus of the preoptic area in prenatally stressed and non-stressed rats, *Brain Research* 370, 1–10

Andersson, T., Magnusson, D. and Wennberg, P. (1997) Early aggressiveness and hyperactivity as indicators of adult alcohol problems and criminality: a prospective longitudinal study of male subjects, *Studies on Crime and Crime Prevention* 6(1), 7–20

APA (American Psychological Association) (2002) New code of ethics, *American Psychologist* 57(12), Washington DC, American Psychological Association

Aronson, E. (1999) *The Social Animal* (8th edition), New York, Worth Publishers/WH Freeman & Co

Ashton, H. (2002) Benziodiazepine abuse. In W. Caan and de Belleroche (eds) *Drink, Drugs and Dependence: From Science to Clinical Practice*, London, Routledge

Bandura, A. (1977) *Social Learning Theory*, Englewood Cliffs NJ, Prentice Hall.

Bandura, A. (1986) *Social Foundations of Thought and Action: A Social Cognitive Theory*, Englewood Cliffs NJ, Prentice-Hall

Bandura, A. (1997) *Self-efficacy: The Exercise of Control*, New York, WH Freeman

Bandura, A., Ross, D. and Ross, S.A. (1963) Vicarious reinforcement and imitative learning, *Journal of Abnormal and Social Psychology* 67, 601–7

Banyard, P. (1996) *Applying Psychology to Health*, London, Hodder & Stoughton

Bell, A.P., Weinberg, M.S. and Hammersmith, S.K. (1981) *Sexual Preference: Its Development in Men and Women*, Bloomington IN, Indiana University Press

Beloff, J. (1993) *Parapsychology: A Concise History*, London, Athlone Press

Bem, D.J. and Honorton, C. (1994) Does psi exist? Replicable evidence for an anomalous process of information transfer, *Psychological Bulletin* 115, 4–18

Bem, D.J., Palmer, J. and Broughton, R.S. (2001) Updating the ganzfeld database: a victim of its own success, *Journal of Parapsychology* 65, 207–18

Blackburn, R. (1993) *The Psychology of Criminal Conduct: Theory, Research and Practice*, Chichester, John Wiley & Sons Ltd

Berndt, T.J (1981) Relations between social cognition, non-social cognition and social behaviour: the case of friendship. In J.H Flavell and L.D Ross (eds) *Social Cognitive Development: Frontiers and Possible Futures*, New York, Cambridge University Press

Bieber, I., Dain, H.J., Dince, P.R., Drellich, M.G., Grand, H.G., Grundlach, R.H., Kremer, M.W., Rifkin, A.H., Wilbur, C.B. and Bieber, T.B. (1962) *Homosexuality: A Psychoanalytic Study*, New York, Basic Books

Blackmore, S. and Troscianko, T. (1985) Belief in the paranormal: probability judgements, illusory control and the 'chance baseline shift', *British Journal of Psychology* 76, 459–68

Blackmore, S. (1985) The adventures of a psi-inhibitory experimenter. In P. Kurtz (ed.) *A Skeptic's Handbook of Parapsychology*, Buffalo, NY, Prometheus Books, 425–48

Blackmore, S. (1997) Probability misjudgement and belief in the paranormal: a newspaper survey, *British Journal of Psychology* 88, 683–9

Blake, S.M., Amaro, H., Schwartz, P.M. and Flinchbaugh, L.J. (2001) A review of substance abuse prevention interventions for young adolescent girls, *Journal of Early Adolescence* 21(3), 294–324

Blumstein, P.W. and Schwartz, P. (1977) Bisexuality: some social psychological issues, *Journal of Social Issues* 33, 30–45

BMA (British Medical Association) (1997) *The Misuse of Drugs*, Amsterdam, Harwood Academic Publishers

Bootzin, R.R., Acocella, J.R. and Alloy, L.B. (1993) *Abnormal Psychology: Current Perspectives*, New York, McGraw-Hill

Bordnick, P.S. (1996) Evaluating the relative efficacy of three aversion therapies designed to reduce craving among male cocaine abusers (Dissertation Abstracts International Section A), *Humanities & Social Sciences* 56(10-A), 4145

Bourne, P.G. (1974) *Addiction*, New York, Academic Press

Bowlby, J. (1944) Forty-four Juvenile Thieves, *International Journal of Psychoanalysis* 25, 1–57

Box, S. (1983) *Deviance, Reality and Society*, London, Tavistock

Brannon, L. and Feist, J. (1992) *Health Psychology: An Introduction to Behaviour and Health*, Belmont CA, Wadsworth

Braud, W.G. (1975) Psi-conducive states, *Journal of Communication* 25(1), 142–52

Brehm, S.S. and Kassin, S.M. (1996) *Social Psychology* (3rd edition), Boston MA, Houghton Mifflin Company

Budney, A.J. and Higgins, S.T. (1998) Therapy Manuals for Drug Addiction (Manual 2) A Community Reinforcement Plus Vouchers Approach: Treating Cocaine Addiction, Maryland, NIDA

Buss, D.M. (1989) Sex differences in human mate preferences: evolutionary hypotheses tested in 37 cultures, *Behavioural and Brain Sciences* 12, 1–14

Buss, D.M. and Schmitt, D.P. (1993) Sexual strategies theory: an evolutionary perspective on human mating, *Psychological Review* 100, 204–32

Buss, D.M., Larsen, R.J., Westen, D. and Semmelroth, J. (1992) Sex differences in jealousy: evolution, physiology and psychology, *Psychological Science* 3, 251–5

Buunk, B. and Hupka, R.B. (1987) Cross-cultural differences in the elicitation of sexual jealousy, *Journal of Sex Research* 23, 12–22

Caan, W. (2002) The nature of heroin and cocaine dependence. In W. Caan and de Belleroche (eds) *Drink, Drugs and Dependence: From Science to Clinical Practice*, London, Routledge

Canter, D. (1989) Offender Profiling, *The Psychologist* 2, 2–16

Canter, D. (1994) *Criminal Shadows: Inside the Mind of the Serial Killer*, London, HarperCollins

Carlson, N.R. (1993) *Psychology: The Science of Behaviour* (4th edition), Boston MA, Allyn & Bacon

Cavadino, M. and Dignan, J. (1997) *The Penal System: An Introduction* (2nd edition), London, Sage

Chadwick, O., Anderson, H.R., Bland, J.M. and Ramsey, J. (1991) Solvent Abuse: A Population-Based Neuropsychological Study, New York, Springer-Verlag

Chassin, L., Pitts, S.C., DeLucia, C. and Todd, M. (1999) A longitudinal study of children of alcoholics: predicting young adult substance use disorders, anxiety and depression, *Journal of Abnormal Psychology* 108(1), 106–19

Clark, M.S. and Hatfield, E. (1989) An evolutionary perspective on human relationships, *Journal of Psychology and Human Sexuality* 2, 39–55

Clemmer, D. (1958) *The Prison Community*, New York, Holt, Rinehart & Winston

Cloninger, C.R. (1987) Neurogenetic adaptive mechanisms in alcoholism, *Science* 236, 410–16

Crandall, J.E. (1985) Effects of favorable and unfavorable conditions on the psi-missing displacement effect, *Journal of the American Society for Psychical Research* 79, 27–38

Crawford, N. (2002) HIV needs psychology, *Monitor on Psychology* 33(10), Washington DC, APA

Croall, H. (1998) *Crime and Society in Britain*, Harlow, Longman

Cuijpers, P., Jonkers, R., de Weerdt, I. and de Jong, A. (2002) The effects of drug abuse prevention at school: the 'Healthy School and Drugs' project, *Addiction* 97, 67–73

Cullen, J.E. and Seddon, J.W. (1981) The application of a behavioural regime to disturbed young offenders, *Personality and Individual Differences* 2, 285–92

Davidson, R.S. (1985) Behavioral medicine and alcoholism. In N. Schneiderman and J.T. Tapp (eds) *Behavioral Medicine: The Biopsychosocial Approach*, Hillsdale NJ, LEA

Davison, G.C. and Neale, J.M. (2001) *Abnormal Psychology* (8th edition), Chichester, John Wiley

Diamond, A. and Goddard, E. (1995) *Smoking Among Secondary School Children in 1994*, London, HMSO

Dindia, K. and Allen, M. (1992) Sex differences in self-disclosure: A meta-analysis, *Psychological Bulletin* 112, 106–24

Dion, K.K., Berscheid, E. and Walster, E. (1972) What is beautiful is good, *Journal of Personality and Social Psychology* 24, 285–90

DoH (Department of Health) (2002) Drug Use, Smoking and Drinking Among Young People in England in 2001: Preliminary Results, London, DoH

Drugscope (2001) *Drug Abuse Briefing – a Guide to the Non-Medical Use of Drugs in Britain*, London, Drugscope

Drummond, S. (2002) Prevention. In W. Caan and de Belleroche (eds) *Drink, Drugs and Dependence: From Science to Clinical Practice*, London, Routledge

Easthope, G. (1993) Perceptions of the causes of drug use in a series of articles in 'The International Journal of the Addictions', *International Journal of the Addictions* 28(6), 559–69

Elkins, R.L. (1991) An appraisal of chemical aversion (emetic therapy) approaches to alcoholism treatment, *Behaviour Research & Therapy* 29(5), 387–413

Erikson, E. (1963) *Childhood and Society* (2nd edition), New York, Norton

Evans, R.I., Rozelle, R.M., Maxwell, S.E., Raines, B.E., Dill, C.A., Guthrie, T.J., Henderson, A.H. and Hill, D.C. (1981) Social modeling films to deter smoking in adolescents: results of a three-year field investigation, *Journal of Applied Psychology* 66(4), 399–414

Eysenck, H.J. (1970) *The Structure of Human Personality* (3rd edition), London, Methuen

Fabrega, H., Ulrich, R., Pilkonis, P. and Mezzich, J. (1991) On the homogeneity of personality disorder clusters, *Comprehensive Psychiatry* 32(5), 373–86

Farrington, D.P. and Dowds, E.A. (1984) Why does crime decrease?, *Justice of the Peace* 11 (August)

Feindler, E.L., Marriott, S.A. and Iwata, M. (1984) Group anger control training for junior high school delinquents, *Cognitive Therapy and Research* 8, 299–311

Feldman, M.P. (1977) *Criminal Behaviour: A Psychological Analysis*, Chichester, John Wiley

Festinger, L., Schachter, S. and Back, K.W. (1950) *Social Pressures in Informal Groups: A Study of Human Factors in Housing*, New York, Harper

Field-Smith, M.E., Bland, J.M., Taylor, J.C., Ramsey, J.D. and Anderson, H.R. (2002) *Trends in Death Associated with Abuse of Volatile Substances*, London, St George's Hospital Medical School (available online at http:/www.vsareport.org)

Fisher, J.D. and Byrne, D. (1975) Too close for comfort: sex differences in response to invasions of personal space, *Journal of Personality and Social Psychology* 32, 15–21

Flay, B. (1985) Psychosocial approaches to smoking prevention: a review of findings, *Health Psychology* 4(5), 449–88

Flay, B.R., Ryan, K.B., Best, J.A., Brown, K.S., Kersell, M.W., D'Avernas, J.R. and Zanna, M.P. (1985) Are social-psychological smoking prevention programs effective? The Waterloo Study, *Journal of Behavioral Medicine* 8, 37–59

Flora, J.A. and Thoreson, C.E. (1988) Reducing the risk of AIDS in adolescents, *American Psychologist* (Special Issue: Psychology and AIDS) 43(11), 965–70

Flory, K., Lynam, D., Milich, R., Leukefeld, C. and Clayton, R. (2002) The relations among personality, symptoms of alcohol and marijuana abuse and symptoms of comorbid psychopathology: results from a community sample, *Experimental & Clinical Psychopharmacology* 10(4), 425–34

Foucault, M. (1977) *Discipline and Punish: The Birth of the Prison*, London, Allen

Frankland, J. (1998) Tobacco use among young people: a review of research and recommendations. In M. Bloor and F. Wood (eds) *Addictions and Problem Drug Use: Issues in Behaviour Policy and Practice*, London, Jessica Kingsley Publishers

Frawley, P.J. and Smith, J.W. (1990) Chemical aversion therapy in the treatment of cocaine dependency as part of a multimodal treatment program: treatment outcome, *Journal of Substance Abuse Treatment* 7, 21–9

Freud, S. (1930) *New Introductory Lectures on Psychoanalysis*, Harmondsworth, Penguin

Gallup, G.H. and Newport, F. (1991) Belief in paranormal phenomena among adult Americans, *Skeptical Inquirer* 15, 137–46

Garland, D. (1994) The development of British criminology. In Maguire, M., Morgan, R. and Reiner, R. (eds) *The Oxford Handbook of Criminology*, Oxford, Oxford University Press

Garnier, H.E. and Stein, J.A. (2002) An 18-year model of family and peer effects on adolescent drug use and delinquency, *Journal of Youth & Adolescence* 31(1), 45–56

Gilligan, C. (1982) *In a Different Voice: Psychological Theory and Women's Development*, Cambridge MA, Harvard University Press

Girden, E. (1962) A review of psychokinesis, *Psychological Bulletin* 59, 353–88

Gleitman, H., Fridlund, A.J. and Reisberg, D. (1999) *Basic Psychology* (5th edition), New York, Norton

Glueck, S. and Glueck, E. (1950) *Unravelling Juvenile Delinquency*, New York, Harper & Row

Goffman, E. (1961) *Asylums*, Harmondsworth, Penguin

Goldstein, A.P. (1986) Psychological skill training and the aggressive adolescent. In S.J. Apter and A.P. Goldstein (eds) *Youth Violence: Programs and Prospects*, New York, Plenum

Goring, C.B. (1913) *The English Convict: A Statistical Study*, London, HMSO

Grad, B., Cadoret, R.J. and Paul, G.I. (1961) The influence of an unorthodox method of wound healing in mice, *International Journal of Parapsychology* 3, 5–24

Gray, D., Saggers, S., Sputore, B. and Bourbon, D. (2000) What works? A review of evaluated alcohol misuse interventions among Aboriginal Australians, *Addiction* 95(1), 11–22

Griffin, K.W., Scheier, L.M., Botvin, G.J. and Diaz, T. (2001) Protective role of personal competence skills in adolescent substance use: psychological well-being as a mediating factor, *Psychology of Addictive Behaviors* 15(3), 194–203

Griffiths, M.D. (1995) *Adolescent Gambling*, London, Routledge

Gurney, E., Myers, F.W.H. and Podmore, F. (1886) *Phantasms of the Living*, London, Trubner

Hansen, L.J., de Fine Olivarius, N., Beich, A., Barfod, S. (1999) Encouraging GPs to undertake screening and a brief intervention in order to reduce problem drinking: a randomized controlled trial, *Family Practice* 16(6), 551–7

Haraldsson, E. and Houtkooper, J. (1992) Effects of perceptual defensiveness, personality and belief on extrasensory perception tasks, *Personality and Individual Differences* 13, 1085–96

Harris, J.R. (1998) *The Nurture Assumption: Why Children Turn Out the Way they Do*, New York, Free Press

Hatfield, E. (1988) Passionate and companionate love. In R.J. Sternberg and M.L. Barnes (eds) *The Psychology of Love*, New Haven CT, Yale University Press

Hatfield, E. and Rapson, R.L. (1987) Passionate love: new directions in research. In W.H. Jones and D. Perlman (eds) *Advances in Personal Relationships*, Greenwich, CT, JAI Press

Hatfield, E., Greenberger, E., Traupmann, J. and Lambert, P. (1982) Equity and sexual satisfaction in recently married couples, *Journal of Sex Research* 18, 18–32

Hatfield, E., Sprecher, S., Pillemer, J.T., Greenberger, D. and Wexler, P. (1989) Gender differences in what is desired in the sexual relationship, *Journal of Psychology and Human Sexuality* 1, 39–52

Hazelwood, R.R. (1987) Analysing the rape and profiling the offender. In R.R. Hazelwood and A.W. Burgess (eds) *Practical Aspects of Rape Investigation: A Multidisciplinary Approach*, New York, Elsevier

Healy, W. and Bronner, A.F. (1936) *New Light on Delinquency and its Treatment*, New Haven CT, Yale University Press

Heider, F. (1958) *The Psychology of Interpersonal Relations*, New York, Wiley

Helzer, J.E. and Canino, G.J. (eds) (1992) *Alcoholism in North America, Europe and Asia*, London, Oxford University Press

Hendrick, S.S. and Hendrick, C. (1995) Gender differences and similarities in sex and love, *Personal Relationships* 2, 55–65

Hess, E. (1975) *The Tell-tale Eye*, New York, Van Nostrand Reinhold

Hill, C.T., Rubin, Z. and Peplau, L.A. (1975) Breakups before marriage: the end of 103 affairs, *Journal of Social Issues* 32, 147–68

Hill, G. (1998) *Advanced Psychology through Diagrams*, Oxford, Oxford University Press

Hollin, C.R. (1989) *Psychology and Crime: An Introduction to Criminological Psychology*, London, Routledge

Homans, G.C. (1961) *Social Behaviour*, New York, Harcourt, Brace & World

Honorton, C. (1985) Meta-analysis of psi ganzfeld research: a response to Hyman, *Journal of Parapsychology* 49(1), 51–91

Honorton, C. and Harper, S. (1974) Psi-mediated imagery and ideation in an experimental procedure for regulating perceptual input, *Journal of the American Society for Psychical Research* 68(2), 156–68

Honorton, C., Ferrari, D.C. and Bem, D.J. (1998) Extraversion and ESP performance: a meta-analysis and a new confirmation, *Journal of Parapsychology* 62(3), 255–276

Hutchinson, M. (1988) A thorn in Geller's side, *British and Irish Skeptic* 2(4), 9–11

Hyman, R. (1989) *The Elusive Quarry: A Scientific Appraisal of Psychical Research*, Buffalo NY, Prometheus

Irwin, H.J. (1999) *Introduction to Parapsychology* (3rd edition), London, McFarland & Co.

Janis, I. and Feshbach, S. (1953) Effects of fear-arousing communications, *Journal of Abnormal and Social Psychology* 48, 78–92

Johnson, M. and Haraldsson, E. (1984) The defense mechanism test as a predictor of ESP scores: Icelandic Studies IV and V, *Journal of Parapsychology* 48(3), 185–200

Kaplan, R.M., Sallis, J.F., Patterson, T.L. (1993) *Health and Human Behaviour*, New York, McGraw-Hill

Keil, H.H.J., Herbert, B., Ullman, M. and Pratt, J.G. (1976) Directly observable voluntary PK effects: a survey and tentative interpretation of available findings from Nina Kulagina and other known related cases of recent date, *Proceedings of the Society for Psychical Research* 56, 197–235

Kelley, H.H. (1983) Love and commitment. In H.H. Kelley, E. Berscheid, A. Christenson, J.H. Harvey, T.L. Huston, G. Levinger, E. McClintock, L.A. Peplau and D.R. Peterson, *Close Relationships*, New York, Freeman

Kershaw, C., Chivite-Matthews, N., Thomas, C. and Aust, R. (2001) *The 2001 British Crime Survey, First Results, England and Wales*, Home Office Statistical Bulletin, London, HMSO

Killen, J.D., Robinson, T.N., Haydel, K.F., Hayward, C., Wilson, D.M., Hammer, L.D., Litt, I.F. and Taylor, C.B. (1997) Prospective study of risk factors for the initiation of cigarette smoking, *Journal of Consulting & Clinical Psychology* 65(6), 1011–16

Kinsey, A.C., Pomeroy, W.B. and Martin, C.E. (1948) *Sexual Behaviour in the Human Male*, Philadelphia, Saunders

Kirby, M., Kidd, W., Koubel, F., Barter, J., Hope, T., Kirton, A., Madry, N., Manning, P. and Triggs, K. (2000) *Sociology in Perspective*, AQA edition, Oxford, Heinemann

Lange, J.S. (1931) *Crime as Destiny*, London, Allen & Unwin

Lawrence, A.R. (1993) Gathering in the sheep and goats ... A meta-analysis of forced-choice sheep-goat studies, 1947–1993, *Proceedings of the 36th Annual Convention of the Parapsychological Association*, Toronto, Canada, 75–86

Lee, J.A. (1988) Love-styles. In R.J. Sternberg and M.L. Barnes (eds) *The Psychology of Love*, New Haven CT, Yale University Press

LeVay, S. (1991) A difference in hypothalamic structure between heterosexual and homosexual men, *Science* 253, 1034–7

Li, T-K. and McBride, W.J. (1995) Pharmacogenetic models of alcoholism, *Clinical Neuroscience* 3, 182–8

Lubetkin, B.S. and Fishman, S.T. (1974) Electrical aversion therapy with a chronic heroin user, *Journal of Behavior Therapy & Experimental Psychiatry* 5(2), 193–5

McAdams, D.P. (2000) *The Person: An Integrated Introduction to Personality Psychology*, Fort Worth TX, Harcourt

McAdams, D.P. and Valliant, G.E. (1982) Intimacy motivation and psychosocial adjustment: a longitudinal study, *Journal of Personality Assessment* 46, 586–93

McGue, M. (1999) The behavioural genetics of alcoholism, *Current Directions in Psychological Science* 8, 109–15

McGue, M., Pickens, R.W. and Svikis, D.S. (1992) Sex and age effects on the inheritance of alcohol problems: a twin study, *Journal of Abnormal Psychology* 101(1), 3–17

McGurk, B.J. and McDougall, C. (1981) A new approach to Eysenck's theory of criminality, *Personality and Individual Differences* 2, 338–40

Maddux, J.F. (2000) Addiction or dependence? *Addiction* 95(5), 661–5

Meyer, V. and Chesser, E.S. (1970) *Behaviour Therapy in Clinical Psychiatry*, Oxford, Penguin

Milton, J. and Wiseman, R. (1999a) A meta-analysis of mass-media tests of extrasensory perception, *British Journal of Psychology* 90, 235–40

Milton, J. and Wiseman, R. (1999b) Does psi exist? Lack of replication of an anomalous process of information transfer, *Psychological Bulletin* 125(4), 387–91

Mitchell, L. (1997) Loud, sad or bad: young people's perceptions of peer groups and smoking, *Health Education Research* 12, 1–14

Money, J. and Ehrhardt, A.A. (1972) *Man and Woman, Boy and Girl*, Baltimore MD, Johns Hopkins University Press

Moore, S. (1996) *Investigating Crime and Deviance* (2nd edition), London, Collins Educational

Morgenstern, J., Langenbucher, J., Labouvie, E. and Miller, K.J. (1997) The comorbidity of alcoholism and personality disorders in a clinical population: prevalence and relation to alcohol typology variables, *Journal of Abnormal Psychology* 106(1), 74–84

Muncie, J. and McLaughlin, E. (2001) *The Problem of Crime*, London, Sage

Murstein, B.I. (1987) A clarification and extension of the SVR theory of dyadic pairing, *Journal of Marriage and the Family* 49, 929–33

Naidoo, J. and Wills, J. (1998) *Practising Health Promotion: Dilemmas and Challenges*, London, Bailliere Tindall

Newcomb, T.M. (1961) *The Acquaintance Process*, New York, Holt, Rinehart & Winston

Nolen-Hoeksema, S. (2001) *Abnormal Psychology*, New York, McGraw-Hill

Ogden, J. (2000) *Health Psychology: A Textbook*, Buckingham, Open University Press

Olds, J. and Milner, P. (1954) Positive reinforcement produced by electrical stimulation of septal area and other regions of rat brain, *Journal of Comparative & Physiological Psychology* 47, 419–27

Orme, J.E. (1974) Precognition and time, *Journal of the Society for Psychical Research* 47, 351–65

Orne, M.T. (1962) On the social psychology of the psychological experiment with particular reference to demand characteristics and their implications, *American Psychologist* 17, 776–83

Palmer, J. (1979) A community mail survey of psychic experiences, *Journal of the American Society for Psychical Research* 73, 221–51

Parrott, A.C. (1995) State of the art. Psychoactive drugs of use and abuse: wobble, rave, inhale or crave? *Journal of Psychopharmacology* 9, 390–1

Parrott, A.C. (1999) Does cigarette smoking cause stress? *American Psychologist* 54(10), 817–20

Pennington, D., Smithson, R., McLoughlin, J., Robinson, D. and Boswell, K. (2003) *Advanced Psychology: Child Development, Perspectives and Methods*, London, Hodder & Stoughton

Pennington, D., McLoughlin, J., Robinson, D., Boswell, K., Dancer, L. and Smithson, R. (2002) *Introducing Psychology: Approaches, Topics and Methods*, London, Hodder & Stoughton

Perkins, H.W. and Berkowitz, A.D. (1986) Perceiving the community norms of alcohol use among students: some research implications for campus alcohol education programming, *International Journal of the Addictions* 21, 961–76

Perkins, H.W., Meilman, P.W., Leichliter, I.S., Cashin, M.A. and Presley, C.A. (1999) Misperceptions of the norms for the frequency of alcohol and other drug use on college campuses, *Journal of American College Health* 47, 253–8

Peters, T.J. and Preedy, V.R. (2002) Alcohol and genetic predisposition. In W. Caan and de Belleroche (eds) *Drink, Drugs and Dependence: From Science to Clinical Practice*, London, Routledge

Phillips, A.G., Coury, A., Fiorino, D., LePiane, F.G., Brown, E. and Fibiger, H.C. (1992) Self-stimulation of the ventral tegmental area enhances dopamine release in the nucleus accumbens: a microdialysis study. In P.W. Kalivas and H.H. Samson (eds) *The Neurobiology of Drug and Alcohol Addiction. Annals of the New York Academy of Sciences*, Vol. 654, New York, New York Academy of Sciences, 199–206

Pinel, J.P.J. (2003) *Biopsychology* (5th edition), Boston, Allyn & Bacon

Plomin, R. (1990) *Nature and Nurture: An Introduction to Behavioral Genetics*, Pacific Grove CA, Brooks/Cole

Prochaska, J.O., DiClemente, C.C. and Norcross, J.C. (1992) In search of how people change: applications to addictive behaviours, *American Psychologist* 47, 1102–14

Radin, D.I. and Ferrari, D.C. (1991) Effects of consciousness on the fall of dice: a meta-analysis, *Journal of Scientific Exploration* 5, 61–83

Radin, D.I. and Nelson, R.D. (1989) Evidence for conscious-related anomalies in random physical systems, *Foundations of Physics* 19(12), 1499–1514

Radin, D.I. and Rebman, J.M. (1996) Are phantasms fact or fantasy? A preliminary investigation of apparitions invoked in the laboratory, *Journal of the Society for Psychical Research* 61, 319–46

Rankin, H., Hodgson, R. and Stockwell, T. (1983) Cue exposure and response prevention with alcoholics: a controlled trial, *Behaviour Research and Therapy* 21, 435–46

Reber, A.S. (2001) *A Dictionary of Psychology* (3rd edition), London, Penguin

Reed, M.D. and Rountree, P.W. (1997) Peer pressure and adolescent substance use, *Journal of Quantitative Criminology* 13(2), 143–80

Rhine, L.E. (1953) Subjective forms of spontaneous psi experiences, *Journal of Parapsychology* 17, 77–114

Rhine, L.E. (1954) Frequency of types of experience in spontaneous precognition, *Journal of Parapsychology* 18, 93–123

Rhine, L.E. (1956) The relationship of agent and percipient in spontaneous telepathy, *Journal of Parapsychology* 20, 1–32

Rhine, L.E. (1961) *Hidden Channels of the Mind*, New York, Morrow

Rhine, L.E. (1963a) Spontaneous physical effects and the psi process, *Journal of Parapsychology* 27, 172–99

Rhine, L.E. (1963b) Auditory psi experience: hallucinatory or physical? *Journal of Parapsychology* 27, 182–98

Richmond, R.L. and Anderson, P. (1994) Research in general practice for smokers and excessive drinkers in Australia and the UK: III. Dissemination of interventions, *Addiction* 89(1), 49–62

Robinson, T.E. and Berridge, K.C. (2000) The psychology and neurobiology of addiction: an incentive-sensitization view, *Addiction* 95 (Suppl. 2), S91–S117

Rosenstock, I.M. (1966) Why people use health services, *Millbank Memorial Fund Quarterly* 44, 94–124

Rubin, Z. (1970) Measurement of romantic love, *Journal of Personality and Social Psychology* 16, 265–73

Rubin, Z. (1973) *Liking and Loving*, New York, Holt, Rinehart & Winston

Rusbult, C.E. (1983) A longitudinal test of the investment model: the development (and deterioration) of satisfaction and commitment in heterosexual involvement, *Journal of Personality and Social Psychology* 45, 101–17

Rusbult, C.E. and Zembrodt, I.M. (1983) Responses to dissatisfaction in romantic involvements: a multidimensional scaling analysis, *Journal of Experimental Social Psychology* 19, 274–93

Sarafino, E.P. (1990) *Health Psychology: Biopsychosocial Interactions*, Chichester, John Wiley & Sons

Schachter, S. (1959) *The Psychology of Affiliation*, Stanford, Stanford University Press

Schaffer, H.R. and Callender, W.M. (1959) Psychologic effects of hospitalization in infancy, *Pediatrics* 24, 528–39

Schuckit, M.A. (1985) Genetics and the risk for alcoholism, *Journal of the American Medical Association* 254, 2614–17

Schuckit, M.A. (1995) *Drug and Alcohol Abuse: A Clinical Guide to Diagnosis and Treatment*, New York, Plenum

Schuckit, M.A., Daeppen, J.B., Tipp, J.E. and Hesselbrock, V.M. (1995) The histories of withdrawal convulsions and delirium tremens in 1648 alcohol dependent subjects, *Addiction* 90, 1335–47

Sheldon, W.H. (1942) *The Varieties of Temperament: A Psychology of Constitutional Differences*, New York, Harper & Row

Siegel, S., Hinson, R.E., Krank, M.D. and McCully, J. (1982) Heroin 'overdose' death: contribution of drug-associated environmental cues, *Science* 216, 436–7

Seivewright, N. and Dougal, W. (1993) Withdrawal symptoms from high dose benzodiazepines in polydrug users, *Drug and Alcohol Dependence* 32, 15–23

Sigall, H. and Ostrove, N. (1973) Beautiful but dangerous: effects of offender attractiveness and nature of the crime on juridic judgement, *Journal of Personality and Social Psychology* 31(3), 410–14

Simpson, J.A. and Gangestad, S.W. (1991) Individual differences in sociosexuality: evidence for convergent and discriminant validity, *Journal of Personality and Social Psychology* 60, 870–83

Skinner, B.F. (1953) *Science and Human Behaviour*, New York, Macmillan

Stacy, A.W., Newcomb, M.D. and Bentler, P.M. (1992) Interactive and higher-order effects of social influences on drug use, *Journal of Health & Social Behavior* 33(3), 226–41

Stead, M., Hastings, G.B. and Tudor-Smith, C. (1996) Preventing adolescent smoking: a review of options, *Health Education Journal* 48, 55–64

Stein, J.A., Newcomb, M.D. and Bentler, P.M. (1987) An 8-year study of multiple influences on drug use and drug use consequences, *Journal of Personality & Social Psychology* 53(6), 1094–1105

Sternberg, R.J. (1986) A triangular theory of love, *Psychological Review* 93, 119–35

Stevenson, I. and Pratt, J.G. (1969) Further investigations of the psychic photography of Ted Serios, *Journal of the American Society for Psychical Research* 63(4), 352–64

Stewart, J., de Wit, H. and Eikelboom, R. (1984) Role of unconditioned and conditioned drug effects in the self-administration of opiates and stimulants, *Psychological Review* 91(2), 251–68

Storm, L. and Thalbourne M.A. (2000) A paradigm shift away from the ESP–PK dichotomy: the theory of psychopraxia, *Journal of Parapsychology* 64(3), 279–300

Stowell, M.S. (1997) Precognitive dreams: a phenomenological study. Part I: methodology and sample cases, *Journal of the American Society for Psychical Research* 91(3), 163–220

Suedfeld, P. (1982) Aloneness as a healing experience. In L.A. Peplau and D. Perlman (eds) *Loneliness: A Sourcebook of Current Theory, Research and Therapy*, New York, Wiley

Sutherland, E.H. (1939) *Principles of Criminology*, Philadelphia PA, Lippincott

Sutherland, E.H. (1947) *Principles of Criminology* (4th edition), Philadelphia PA, Lippincott

Taylor, S.P. and Leonard, K.E. (1983) Alcohol and human physical aggression. In R.G. Green and E.I. Donnerstein (eds) *Aggression: Theoretical and Empirical Reviews (Vol. 2)* New York, Academic Press, 77–101

Thalbourne, M.A. (1981) Extraversion and the sheep-goat variable: a conceptual replication, *Journal of the American Society for Psychical Research* 75(2), 105–19

Thalbourne, M.A. and Haraldsson, E. (1980) Personality characteristics of sheep and goats, *Personality & Individual Differences* 1(2), 180–5

Thomason, I.G. and Rathod, N.H. (1968) Aversion therapy for heroin dependence, *Lancet* 2(7564), 382–4

Tomkins, S.S. (1968) Psychological models for smoking behavior, *Review of Existential Psychology & Psychiatry* 8(1), 28–33

Turvey, B.E. (1996) *Behaviour Evidence: Understanding Motives and Developing Suspects in Unsolved Serial Rapes Through Behavioural Profiling Techniques*, Knowledge Solutions, www.corpus-delicti.com

Wagner, M.W. and Monnet, M. (1979) Attitudes of college professors toward extra-sensory perception, *Zetetic Scholar* 5, 7–17

Wallace, P., Cutler, S. and Haines, A. (1988) Randomised control trial of general practitioner intervention in patients with excessive alcohol consumption, *British Medical Journal* 287, 663ff.

Walster, E. (1965) The effect of self esteem on romantic liking, *Journal of Experimental Social Psychology* 1, 184–97

Walster, E., Aronson, V., Abrahams, D. and Rottman, L (1966) The importance of physical attractiveness in dating behaviour, *Journal of Personality and Social Psychology* 4, 508–16

Watt, C. (2001) Paranormal cognition. In R. Roberts and D. Groome, (eds) *Parapsychology: The Psychology of Unusual Experience*, London, Arnold, 130–40

Weber, A.L. (1992) *Social Psychology*, London, Harper Perennial

West, R. (2001) Theories of addiction, *Addiction* 96(1), 3–13

Wheeler, S. (1961) Socialization in correctional communities, *American Sociological Review* 26, 697

Williams, K.S. (1991) *Textbook on Criminology*, London, Blackstone Press Ltd

Winger, G., Hofmann, F.G. and Woods, J.H. (1992) Handbook on Drug and Alcohol Abuse, New York, Oxford University Press

Wiseman, R., Watt, C., Stevens, P., Greening, E. and O'Keefe, C. (in press) Investigations into alleged hauntings, *British Journal of Psychology*

Wollheim, R. (1991) *Freud* (2nd edition), London, Fontana Press

Woolf, H. and Tumim, S. (1991) *Prison Disturbances April 1990*, Cm 1456, London, HMSO

World Health Organization (1997) *Tobacco or Health: A Global Status Report*, WHO

Wright, P.H. (1982) Men's friendships, women's friendships and the alleged inferiority of the latter, *Sex Roles* 8, 1–20

Zimbardo, P., Hancy, C. and Banks, C. (1973) Interpersonal dynamics in a simulated prison, *International Journal of Criminology and Penology* 1, 69–97

Zucker, R.A., Ellis, D.A., Fitzgerald, H.E. and Bingham, C.R. (1996) Other evidence for at least two alcoholism II. Life course variation in antisociality and heterogeneity of alcoholic outcome, *Development & Psychopathology* 8(4), 831–48

# Index